HE SHROPSHIRE HILLS

On Caer Caradoc

THE SHROPSHIRE HILLS

A Walker's Guide

by

DAVID HUNTER

CICERONE PRESS
MILNTHORPE, CUMBRIA

ISBN 1 85284 064 1
© David Hunter 1991

Text: David Hunter
Sketch plans: Vera Hunter
Photography: David and Vera Hunter

Acknowledgements

To my wife for reading and checking every word,
walking every step of the way, identifying wild flowers
and patience above and beyond the call of duty.

Preface

IN THIS tight little island of ours there is an astonishing variety of beautiful scenery, much of which remains unknown.

One such area is that of the Shropshire Hills and Severn Valley which provides much good and varied walking well within the capabilities of most people. It is a part of the country held in great affection by those who know it, but it seems clear that many people are unaware of the pleasures that could be awaiting them. This book, whilst not aiming to be an all embracing encyclopaedia on walking and exploring in this particularly attractive region between the Midlands and the Welsh Border, aims to distil a little of the essence by way of a series of walks across the area.

Contents

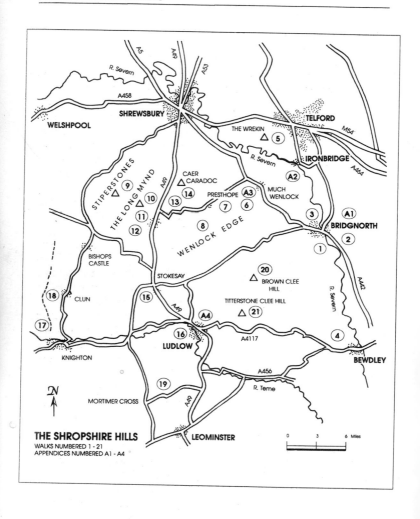

THE SHROPSHIRE HILLS
WALKS NUMBERED 1 - 21
APPENDICES NUMBERED A1 - A4

Introduction

THE TERRITORY to be explored is the Area of Outstanding Natural Beauty in South Shropshire bisected by the A49 and centred on the little town of Church Stretton. No hard and fast rules are set, for we shall stray beyond these boundaries to visit Bridgnorth, a town neglected by many tourists, to enjoy the pleasures of the River Severn. Nor are we confined to the county of Shropshire, for we shall indulge in a little trespass into neighbouring Hereford and Worcester to walk through the ancient Wyre Forest and sample Bewdley's river scenery.

The pleasures of river walking will be contrasted with the high moors of the Long Mynd, the sharp rocky spine of the Stiperstones, and the long windy ridge of Wenlock Edge. There is a magic ring to the very names of these places, and many have strong historical connections. At Knighton we shall be nudging into the Welsh Borders as Offa's Dyke is walked. The Clee Hills will provide us with the highest point in Shropshire, at 1772 feet, and here and there will be uncovered old superstitions, some not quite dead.

Much of the area is sparsley populated, and the names on the map may only indicate a remote hamlet or tiny village that happily has not grown with the times. Nor are the towns over large; their streets, pages in the book of architectural history, are a delight to explore: Ludlow is a prime example.

The landscape was shaped millions of years ago, it rises and falls in great rolling waves, and the walker may head off on a long ridge and enjoy the unfolding view as he rides the wave crest or plunges deep into the trough of the valley. The remains of ancient mining, as far back as Roman times, will be encountered and he can share a windy hill top with the ghosts of our long dead Celtic forebears. If you think this is stretching the imagination a little too far, then suspend judgement until you stand on Caer Caradoc.

There is more than the hills and river valleys to be explored. There are the castles of Ludlow, Clun, Hopton and Stokesay; the little village churches and the ancient priory at Much Wenlock. From the Wrekin's lonely summit the walker can look towards the birthplace of the famous iron foundries of Ironbridge, home of the Industrial Revolution. Ironbridge needs a day to itself at the very least, with its wealth of history; it is unquestionably one of the finest days out for all the family in the Midlands.

It is not only the past that can be enjoyed. There are other delights, not so easily located, less certain in the timing of their experience, but equally lasting in the mind of memorable days' walking. The swift blue flash of a kingfisher speeding across the brown waters of the Severn or the sight of a heron, that most patient of fishermen, standing as still as a garden ornament by the waters of a little brook. To this add the thrill of seeing the high soaring buzzards hunting along the scarp or catching a glimpse of a small group of deer, those elusive shadows of the forest.

All this is just to sketch in the scene, to whet the appetite but attention must be given to the logistics of getting there, being properly equipped to enjoy the day and not being unduly burdened with the anxieties of finding the way.

GETTING THERE

THOSE WITH their own transport will not be faced with any problem, but those without a car do not have too great a disadvantage. A little careful homework on local travel facilities is of course essential, but this is made easy by an excellent publication, "Shropshire Bus and Train Guide". It has an easily read map showing all routes with the appropriate numbers, clearly distinguishing between services that operate 5 days per week or more and those which are less frequent. Published by the County Council it is backed up by Travel Centres at Oswestry, Shrewsbury and Telford. Timetables are available from these centres and libraries. Telephone enquiries: 0345 056785 (Mon-Fri 8.30-5.45 and Sat 8.30-5pm). It is also useful to note that there are British Rail stations at Shrewsbury, Church Stretton, Craven Arms, and Ludlow. Nor should the Severn Valley Railway by forgotten, operating between Bridgnorth and Kidderminster: it will receive more detailed attention later.

MAPS

THE RELEVANT sheet number of the Ordnance Survey map is

The Long Mynd

given for each walk and it is recommended that you carry it with you on the outing. It will allow for changes of route, extending or curtailing a walk to suit the day's conditions. It is also helpful in planning other expeditions if crossing paths, not on the scheduled route, are checked for quality and destination. One of the many pleasures of walking is the time spent sitting on a hilltop with map spread over the knees picking out distant landmarks, putting a name to a misty hilltop or village spire.

Excellent as the OS Maps are they cannot guarantee easy walking. Paths that are writ large upon the map are sometimes ill defined on the ground, have been subject to diversion, or having fallen into disuse have been replaced by unofficial but locally accepted alternatives. No map maker however good can totally keep up with the changes. The best map for the walker is undoubtedly the 1/25,000 scale, $2^{1}/_{2}$ inches to the mile. It provides an immense amount of detail and is particularly useful in determining the passage of paths through fields, for example, by clearly showing which side of a boundary fence the walker can legally follow.

The obvious adjunct to navigating is a compass. At first sight this may not seem all that essential, but I have used this as much in the lower hills and in forest walking as I have in the high fells of the Lake District. A little time spent learning the principles of map reading and compass navigation will pay rich dividends, avoiding the frustrations, not to say embarrassment, of getting lost. The best of walkers stray from their intended path on occasion but intelligent use of the map will quickly correct the situation. I am fond of saying "You are not lost if you know where you are".....a self evident truth you may think but experienced walkers will know exactly what I mean. Remember also that some of the walks described are in upland areas where low cloud and mist can envelop the walker and obscure landmarks. Here is just the situation where carrying a compass and having the confident ability to use it is very reassuring.

WAYMARKING AND SIGNPOSTING

IT IS the practice to mark the points where footpaths or bridleways leave the road with metal or wooden signs. In some parts of the country local authorities have followed this procedure with commendable attention to detail, every path is signposted; an immense help to the walker and not without benefit to farmers and landowners. In Shropshire a great many paths are not yet indicated in this way. Whilst walking in the Bridgnorth area I found five examples of unsigned footpaths within a mile or two. Here again the map solves the problem. I asked the County Council's Rights of Way Officer to comment on the signing of footpaths and he replied as follows; "Shropshire's signposting is not as well advanced as some counties but it is catching up fast. During 1989 the County Council erected more than 1250 posts. At this rate all paths should be signed by the year 2000. The policy at present is to do all paths on a parish by parish basis. Inevitably this will mean that some areas will not be signed for a while yet to come. Unless challenged, walkers should assume that the rights of way are as shown on current OS maps, irrespective of whether they lack signposts or waymarks". Useful advice and encouraging news.

Waymarking of a path is sometimes found throughout its length. Many counties have all their popular paths so indicated. Shropshire is not so well endowed, but the marks that will be found are yellow arrows for footpaths and blue arrows for bridleways. Additionally certain routes may carry special waymarking. National Trails (we used to call them Long Distance Paths) under the auspices of the Countryside Commission, carry their now famous acorn symbol. In our area of exploration the Offa's Dyke path is so marked. Another long distance path that includes part of our area is The Shropshire Way, a combined project by the local rambling organisations and the County Council. (Not adopted by the Countryside Commission at time of writing.)

WHAT TO WEAR

THE OUTDOOR leisure clothing industry has produced a wide variety in price and style of apparel. A common sense approach will provide the equipment suitable to the purpose and pocket. The aim is to be comfortable at all times - keeping cool, keeping warm, keeping dry and yet not being overloaded. The secret of comfortable walking is in being well shod and having layers of clothing that are easily put on or stored away in the rucksack.

A medium sized rucksack should suit most needs, although family walkers with young children may favour one of the larger framed variety. The proper packing and strap adjustment is a great aid to comfort. Apart from food and drink, you should carry some basic first aid equipment - sting relief, insect repellent, sticking plaster, crepe bandage and the like. A small torch should be considered where daylight hours are short and a whistle for emergency use, six short blasts, six long blasts.

What to wear is a matter of individual taste but knee breeches are a very comfortable garment, and the accompanying long stockings take the brunt of the splashed mud, so reducing washing. Light or heavyweight shirts according to season, preferably with pockets, and a good v-necked jumper, together with waterproof anorak and leggings are all necessary requirements. Headgear, even if you normally go hatless, is important, woolly bobble hats for winter and a floppy hat as a protection on those occasions when the sun suggests that we are in warmer climes than that to which we are generally accustomed.

Footwear is the single item that requires most care in selection. Whilst strong shoes will do for some of the walks, boots are generally needed. If you are buying for the first time don't be put off by the high prices of some specialist makers. Excellent as their products are you do not need to buy at the top of the range to find perfectly satisfactory boots that, with proper care, will give long service. The purchaser should look for padded ankle tops, sewn in tongues, quick release laces and good sole grips. Take your time when in the shop, checking for all the points mentioned and search for any unevenness or protruding nails which will become quickly apparent after a mile or two's walking. Despite the difficulty there may be in fully waterproofing some light weight boots, I go for these where conditions are not going to be over muddy ground reserving my medium weight leather boots for winter walking. Leather is not in itself waterproof, but regular attention with Nikwax and similar products should ensure dry feet. Wet feet in summer can be endured, on a frosty winter's day it is quite another matter.

CHILDREN

CHILDREN OF all ages enjoy the adventure of a country walk and their stamina is surprising, but don't overstretch them. Toddlers and young babies are sometimes transported in papoose carriers.

These are very useful in liberating young parents and allowing them to pursue the pleasures of country walking and are little more trouble than carrying a rucksack. There are however dangers, whilst the exercise may be keeping you at a comfortable temperature, the static child can become cold to the extent of hypothermia. Likewise over-exposure to the sun has obvious dangers; sensible clothing and regular checks avoids the problem.

WHEN TO WALK

THE ROUTES described in this book can be followed throughout the year subject to extremes of weather, such as the extensive flooding that sometimes occurs along the Severn, or possibly dangerous snowfalls in the hills. Each season has its offering and there are not many days in the year when a walk is totally out of the question. The light breezes of spring, with the greening of the trees and the fresh wild flowers is a delightful time of the year. Summer brings blue skies, high white clouds and the colours of the ripening harvest. Autumn, perhaps one of the best seasons for the walker with its dramatic colouring of trees heather and bracken, leads one to the pleasures of winter walking. The shorter days produce their own particular pleasures: the crunch of boot over frost hardened ground, stormy skies add interest to the landscape and woods freed from the veil of their foliage give up some of their secrets, whilst the study of tracks left in soft mud may give hope of the sight of deer round the next corner - in this connection to travel silently is to travel hopefully.

We learn as we go, becoming self taught in elements of bird recognition, wild life and related nature study. Walkers with an enquiring mind will gradually acquire a small library of books. Amongst those that I have found useful are the Collins Field Guides to Trees, Birds, Insects and Mammals and similar publications. The *AA Book of the Countryside* is packed with a wealth of information and its wild flower key is a particularly good starting point. There are more specialist books, that may find a place in your library as your interest grows.

I find old roads and tracks of particular fascination and often turn to Christopher Taylor's *Roads and Tracks of Britain*, or Sir William Addison's *The Old Roads of England. The Shell Book of English Villages* is full of little pearls of information whilst *The Spur Book of Map and Compass* will help you acquire navigation skills.

Finally, may I recommend a Countryside Commission publication to you. Titled *Out in the Country* it is available from the Publications Department, 19/23 Albert Road, Manchester M19 2EQ. It is free and its 40 pages are full of useful information for both the novice and veteran walker with sections on access to the countryside, wayfinding, rights of way, safety and many other aspects of walking.

Using This Guidebook

In the route descriptions, walking directions are in italic, background details in roman.

1: Severn Down

BASIC ROUTE DETAIL:	Bridgnorth, west side Severn down stream, Daniel's Mill, Hampton Loade (or extension to Highley) return by Severn Valley Railway. Note: check if running. See end of chapter.
MAPS:	1/25,000 S0 69/79 (Pathfinder 911) and S0 68/78. 1/50,000 Landranger Sheet 138.
DISTANCE:	6 miles or 8 miles approx.
CAR PARKING:	Low Town off A442 near Fox Inn.
TOILETS:	Opposite Fox Inn.
TOURIST INFORMATION:	The Library, Listley Street. Bridgnorth Tel: 074 62 3358.

From the car park turn left along the A442 and after short distance turn left again, soon to cross the bridge over the Severn.

The clock tower on the right was erected in 1949 to commemorate the contribution to science and engineering by Richard Trevithick and John Rastrick whose first passenger locomotive engine was built only a short distance away in 1808. Immediately ahead, Bridgnorth's largest advertisement, covering an entire wall, hits you straight in the eye. It carries the proud message that S.E.& A Ridley Ltd., established in 1616, are the oldest firm of seedsmen in Great Britain: supplying clover, grass, root and grain seeds.

As the walker advances over the bridge the prospect of High Town opens up. To the right the sandstone tower of St. Leonard's Church, around which houses are perched on the cliff that falls steeply down towards the river. To the left is Telford's handsome church of St Mary Magdalene. Below, on the river bank, there is always a large congregation of white doves, mallards and some Canada geese enjoying the liberality of the duck feeding public.

Once over the bridge turn left to follow the river, gaining the bank through a small paved park. The Severn is now closely followed all the way to Hampton, with the exception of one small, voluntary diversion. As Castle Mount falls back the Severn Valley Railway's station is seen and

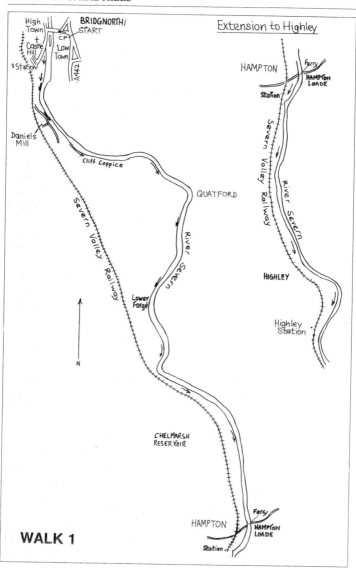

WALK 1

behind that the top of Pan Pudding Hill, leaving little doubt as to the origins of its name.

Bridgnorth is soon left behind. Shortly after passing under the concrete span of the bypass a wooded area is entered but the path keeps close to the river bank. In just over quarter of a mile from the bypass a footbridge takes the walker over a little stream. At this point a turn to the right and over the road will enable a visit to be made to Daniels Mill, the entrance to which is marked by an old millstone.

It is common for a local history to record that "there has been a mill on this site since before Domesday" and Daniel's Mill is no exception. The mill has been in the present owner's family for two hundred years, it was in full time working up to 1957 processing animal feeds. Prior to that it operated as a flour mill. Since the death of the miller in 1957 a great deal of careful restoration work has been done and today the mill is again grinding flour, following the centuries old tradition.

The water to power the mill comes from the Potseething Spring, rising about half a mile away near Coomsley. This spring was reputed to have a mineral content that was soothing to those suffering from sore eyes. The Severn Valley Railway is carried on a viaduct high above the millpond, a good opportunity for photographers if a train is passing. The mill wheel is the largest on a working corn mill in this country. Measuring over 38 feet in diameter and weighing a ton a foot, it clearly needed a fine degree of engineering design and construction to ensure smooth running. Part of our industrial heritage, it is made from cast iron and dates from 1854. It was built at the famous Abraham Darby's Coalbrookdale Forge. The mill is open to the public (details end of chapter) and by way of a souvenir you can buy a bag of stone ground wholemeal flour and have a stab at making your own bread.

After visiting the mill retrace your steps and continue downstream. At first the path is very close to the river edge and as it can be slippery after wet weather, some caution is needed. The path opens up again to more comfortable walking and ahead can be seen the wooded sandstone cliffs of Cliff Copice. The river is busy with wild fowl and the trees edging the river provide a good feeding ground for birds; blue tits and great tits are particularly active. There are kingfishers about and there has not been a single occasion when I have failed to see one, however

19

briefly. Herons are also likely to be seen.

Nearly two miles downstream Quatford, on the opposite bank is passed. Its more visible features include Quatford Castle, a battlemented residence built in 1830 and the high bluff that nudges forward to the river. Long ago its commanding position accommodated a motte and bailey. Beyond it lies the church; what a splendid view there must be from its sandstone tower!

Progressing downstream it is not long before a tall chimney announces the little settlement of Lower Forge now undergoing something of a face lift. On reaching the hamlet a tunnel can be seen cut from the sandstone cliffs, a relic of the days when the forge was busily engaged in the manufacture of nails. The tunnel accommodated a canal cut from Astbury to carry iron ore by narrow boat to the works. The boats were "legged" through the tunnel with the finished product being returned the same way or by horse and cart along the lanes. In recent years a canoeist (bold fellow) attempted a passage through the tunnel but the waterway was partly blocked and he was obliged to haul his canoe over a rock fall.

Charcoal burning was a local occupation and trees in the area were coppiced for the purpose. A small diversion up the track from the river will provide a view of this tiny iron-making settlement. The white building was both the pay office and the manager's house, nearby a row of 8 cottages accommodated the workers. The present owner of the cottages told me that according to his lease he is still obliged to pay two shillings and sixpence per annum for the right of passage for a horse and cart over the farm roads. The largest house, Severn House, is partly built into the sandstone.

Continuing along the bank a bridge over the Mor Brook is crossed and the high banks of the Chelmarsh Reservoir are seen to the right. (There is a nature reserve there but it is only open to members of the Shropshire Wild Life and Ornithological Society.....it is off our route but a board gives details of what may be seen during the course of the year, for the record these may include, January, wild geese and whooper swans. February offers the possibility of goosander, golden eye and widgeon. November promises black terns or a possible osprey. December is busy with hundreds of mallards, with slavonian grebe and red throated diver possible. The marsh area is a habitat for snipe and water rails.)

High tree covered cliffs rise here and there along the river, and little

Looking upstream. The River Severn near Highley

streams add their widow's mite to the waters of the Severn. Near Hampton
Loade a bright blue bridge arches across the river, it is the property of the
Severn Trent Water Authority and not open to the public. This is a pity as

there are a very limited number of bridges and to be able to cross here to join the footpath on the opposite bank would be useful to walkers.

A little further on as Hampton is reached a ferry operates but it cannot be relied upon at all times, since flood conditions may restrict its operation. A bell to summon the ferry is found on a telegraph post, not that we need to cross the river on this excursion, but it offers possibilities in planning future riverside walks.

Just beyond the ferry a lane is reached. This is the point where the walker has to select his options.

Option One

Continue downstream for a further two and a half miles to take the train back (when operating: see end of chapter) from Highley. It is pleasant walking with trees edging the banks here and there. When the Colliery Bridge is reached it is worthwhile leaving the bank for a moment to take in the view from above of the river within its wooded setting. Coal was being mined at the Highley Colliery until the 1960's. At time of writing the spoil heaps across the river are being landscaped as part of a country park project.

The walk continues still on the west bank. Just past the ferry at The Ship Inn a track leads up to the station at Highley and your return by rail.

Option Two

Those who feel that they have now walked far enough should make their way up the lane to Hampton Loade Station for the journey back to Bridgnorth by steam railway.

A railway between Shrewsbury and Worcester was first mooted in 1846 and seven years later the Severn Valley Railway Company was formed. Railway history is all too often a complicated matter, with familiar stories of shortages of money, amalgamations, engineering difficulties, and particularly in the 1960's, closures. Sufficient therefore to say that construction began in 1858 and twenty years on a link to Kidderminster had been established.

As uneconomic lines were closed after the Beeching Report of 1963, Preservation Societies sprang up with the avowed intention of protecting and preserving at least a part of our great railway heritage. (The number of centres is close to the hundred mark).

*Severn Valley Railway - the restored Kidderminster station
based on a design of 1890 for Ross-on-Wye*

The Severn Valley Railway Preservation Society was formed in 1965, operating on sixteen miles of track between Kidderminster and Bridgnorth. Its enterprise encompasses seven stations, carriage and wagon works at Bewdley, with heavy engineering restoration and maintenance sheds at Bridgnorth.

There is a daily timetable in operation from mid-May to mid-September with some services in March, October and around Christmas. Steam Gala days and the Autumn spectacular attract large crowds of enthusiasts from many parts of the country.

Kidderminster station was constructed from a design for the Ross-on-Wye station of 1890, with a Victorian post box nicely setting the date. Enamelled advertising plates clamour for attention proclaiming the merits of some still familiar, and some forgotten, brands.

From Kidderminster the traveller is off on a chugging, gently rumbling adventure, high above the world on embankments, diving deep into cuttings or vanishing into the blackness of Bewdley Tunnel. The scenic route follows the edge of the Wyre Forest, and travellers may be surprised at the sight of bison on the skyline until they discover that they are passing through a Safari Park. Progress is made at a comfortable pace, giving time to enjoy the scenery, even identify some of the wild flowers in the woods and along the embankments. For much of the way it keeps close company with the river with splendid views of the fast flowing Severn.

Stops are made at little country stations, crowded with more passengers than they probably ever saw in their strictly commercial days.

At Bridgnorth, northern terminus of the line, there is freedom to walk round the engine sheds, where the locomotives are maintained and former rusting kings of the iron road are restored to health.

On leaving Bridgnorth station a return to the car park can be made either by ascending the steps to Castle Mount and descending the other side, turning right to walk round the Mount, or take the road up into the town before descending Cartway to the bridge and thus back to Low Town.

PLACES TO VISIT

SEVERN VALLEY RAILWAY: Travel enquiries: Bewdley (0299) 401001. Daily services from about Mid-May to Mid-September with other services earlier and later in the year.

CHILDHOOD AND COSTUME MUSEUM: Postern Gate. Bridgnorth.

BRIDGNORTH MUSEUM: Northgate. Open Easter to September 2-4pm Sats and bank hols.

ST MARY MAGDALENE CHURCH: Open daily.

DANIEL'S MILL: South of Bridgnorth off B4373.
Open Sats & Suns Easter to end Sept.
11am-6pm or dusk whichever is earlier.
Parties should phone Bridgnorth 2753.

DUDMASTON HALL. QUATT: 17th cent. house of Francis Darby of Coalbrookdale, also gardens.
National Trust property. Open April-end Sept.

Wed and Sun only 2-6pm. Closed Bank Holidays. Situated off A442
4 miles south Bridgnorth.

(SEE ALSO LIST END OF NEXT WALK.)

2: High Rock

BASIC ROUTE DETAIL:	Bridgnorth, east bank of Severn down stream, Quatford, Stanmore, Hoccum, Roughton, Burcote Rocks, Rindleford, The Knolls, Batch Lane, High Rock, Hermitage Caves, Low Town.
MAPS:	1/25,000 SO69/79 (Pathfinder 911) 1/50,000 Landranger Sheet 138.
DISTANCE:	11 miles approx.
CAR PARKING:	Low Town off A442 near Fox Inn.
TOILETS:	Opposite Fox Inn.
TOURIST INFORMATION:	The Library, Listley Street, Bridgnorth Tel: 074 62 3358

*From the car park, turn left and in a short distance left again, signposted
to Bridgnorth town centre. On reaching bridge, turn left to follow the River
Severn downstream on eastern bank.*

From the riverside walk there are good views of Castle Hill
beneath which are the caves once used as dwellings. There is one
opening that was intended to serve quite a different purpose.
During the Civil War there was an attempt by the Parliamentarians
to tunnel through the easily worked sandstone into the town: a
venture which probably says more for the enterprise and enthusi-
asm of the besiegers than of their consideration of practical strate-
gies.

The southern end of the island in the river provides a haven for the
wildfowl. The feathered residents include Canada and greylag
geese and the inevitable mallards. The Severn flows swiftly beneath
tall chestnut trees whose branches dip down to the water, making
a green protective canopy for the wildfowl and their young in

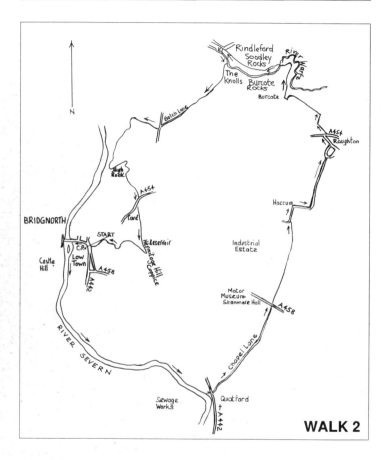

WALK 2

season.

Follow the river, passing under the concrete span of the bypass, until it bends very close to the road at Quatford just over two miles downstream from your starting point. Ahead can be seen the high bluff of Camp Hill and Quatford church. As houses are reached a stile is crossed to take a path sharp left, to reach the road after a few yards, opposite the old post office.

Cross the road and walk up Chapel Lane as it climbs away from the river

Looking out from the Hermitage Caves

soon to leave the village behind. It is a quiet lane edged by woods with sandstone outcropping here and there. The sandstone has been inscribed in a literate, not to say artistic manner with initials, dates, words, even faces and symbols, but their meaning is not clear, leaving a small enigma for the walker to puzzle out as he makes his way uphill. At the top of the hill the views open out to a gently rolling countryside of fields and low wooded hills.

As a T-junction is approached the grounds of Stanmore Hall Camping Park are seen to the right.

The former stable block of the nineteenth century Hall houses the Midland Motor Museum, specialising in sports and sports racing cars and motor cycles. Over a hundred cars, in excellent condition, some still involved in competitive events, are on show, including some of the veterans of the famous pre-war track at Brooklands. Just to mention some of the names is to begin to call the roll of honour of the motor industry....Aston Martin, Bugatti, Ferrari, Jaguar, Morgan, MG and Porsche. The two wheel enthusiasts will encounter equally well known names, AJS. Ariel, Norton, Sunbeam, Triumph, Velocette and Honda. There is also a nature trail, picnic and children's play area. Details of opening times end of chapter.

When the T-junction with the A458 is reached cross the road to join a metalled lane opposite, which soon becomes a wide track. There is open country to the right and for a while the Stanmore Industrial Estate is bordered on the left. This is a sharp demarcation between country and industry, so much so that at one point my attention was divided by the deep red glow of hot metal from a forge on one side and the startled flight of a covey of partridges on the other.

Ignore the turning to the right as the factory sites begin to fall back and maintain your forward direction on a much narrower path with hedge on left and wire fence on right. The path widens again and when a lane is reached go forward towards Hoccum. From here we are following little used lanes giving the flavour of the country roads of the past.

When Hoccum House is reached the lane takes a sharp right turn downhill, eventually to pass a house that still retains an old hand water pump in its front garden. When the road divides, ignore turn to right and continue forward, the garden of the house to the right is full of snowdrops in the early spring.

After passing Willowbrook Cottage on left, a road is reached, turn left to make a junction with the A454. Turn right and cross road. In a few yards join path on the left. This is found at the foot of the steep roadside bank. Head diagonally left across field to stile which is found between two willow trees. Once over stile and tiny brook turn right following path with field boundary on your right. A further waymarked stile is crossed, then turn left along field boundary with hedge on your left. Davenport House is seen on its hill-top site to the north east.

At end of large field pass through metal gate with the path now swinging slightly to the left. At top of slight rise go forward towards gate situated between a cottage and a barn. Once through the gate cross a short grassy paddock and over further stile. Here turn right to take path running behind the cottage. Pause at the stile for a moment to take a look at the brickwork of the barn with its pleasing patterning, worth a photograph if the light is right.

From here on we enter on the best of the walk, passing through similar but in their own ways, quite different environments, with contrasts of scale. One a small, almost secret, river valley, the other the more expansive scenery associated with the Severn.

Take the path that runs behind the cottage with wooded slopes to your left. Soon the walker is following a delightful terraced path high above the little River Worfe. As the path descends, cross waymarked stile and go forward with sandstone cliffs to your left. The path swings round the cliff and the way then crosses the stile by a large gate on left to pass through garden area of a white house, before crossing cattle grid. Go forward on a metalled track to cross river by a small hump backed bridge.

Pause here to take in the scene. You are in a narrow river valley, with the wooded heights of Burcote Rocks and Soudley Rocks walling in the gorge to create one of nature's hidden gardens. The tree lined banks of the river and the woods provide a sheltered habitat for birds. I once watched a heron glide gracefully up the stream to land just a few feet from where I stood.

From the bridge bear left along the track, with the river winding through the valley to your left, to reach Rindleford Mill in a little over half a mile. Do not go beyond the mill, but turn left as it is reached to cross the Worfe by way of a little wooden bridge, no longer in the first flush of youth. Follow the path upstream with the rock outcrops to your right. About two hundred yards from the bridge take a track on the right which makes its way through the woods with high banks on either side.

Hermitage Wood, Bridgnorth

The rising woodland track is followed for half a mile to join Batch Lane which is followed for a quarter of a mile to reach a metalled lane. Here turn left and in a few yards take a signed footpath on right; a wide track as far *as Woodside Cottage where it narrows to run between hedges, busy with blue and great tits. On reaching the wood, about a quarter of a mile from the lane, turn left to follow a narrow but clear path along the inside edge of the wood. After a short distance a junction of paths is reached, take right fork which runs downhill but after only a short distance turn left up a stepped path to follow a narrow terraced path through the centre of the wooded hillside. The slopes to the right fall sharply away with the River Severn glimpsed through the trees, the veil which hides the view will shortly be thrown back as the walker arrives at a high bluff thrust forward to give an exciting prospect of the river.*

It is a superb position with every incentive to stop for refreshment and enjoy the magnificent views at a giddy height above the road with the Severn immediately below. Upstream the river flows under the high wooded cliffs on the east, whilst on the west bank diminutive players people the golf course. Below are the towers of Fort Pendlestone, a fake military-looking building of the mid nineteenth century, built by William Whitmore of Apley Park whose house we shall see, at a distance, on the next walk. Downstream Severn Park is laid out, with little blue and white figures racing towards the matchstick-like posts of the rugby pitch. The eye is carried quickly to Bridgnorth on its commanding height.

At the day's end it is a rewarding place to pause and watch the fiery light of the setting sun spreading a great wash of orange behind the blackly silhouetted Clee Hills beyond Bridgnorth.

When the last of the rocky observation points is reached, the view somewhat occluded by its crown of Scots pine, and the rock much decorated with the initials of Bridgnorth's younger generation, a fish hook turn is made through the woods. From this last high point the path now swings to the left behind the rocky bluff. The terraced path should now be followed, still through the woods. As the path falls a little it bears to the right and then rises again, to join a crossing path coming in from the left, turn right with this. After a hundred yards or so the path divides, take the left fork, (upper path) and continue forward to meet the road, having passed a reservoir on your left.

The road (A454) is reached by a public footpath sign. Cross the busy road to join path opposite which climbs steeply.

Ahead are a series of large caves. Local legend has it that a witch lived in one of these caves and took flight in traditional style each evening as darkness fell.

A rather more famous resident - and with some evidence to substantiate his existence - was a hermit, Ethelred, (or Ethelward); a grandson of Alfred the Great and brother of Athelstan, King of Wessex and Mercia, in AD 925. An inspection of the caves will show evidence of the working of the stone to create a small chapel-like chamber. Alfred's encouragement of learning is well known and it is interesting that this passed down to his grandson who decided to retire to these quiet caves to devote his time to a study of literature.

Having viewed the former retreat of the learned hermit, retrace your steps a few yards to take the path that runs along the inside edge of the wood above the caves.

About 100 yards after passing the green banks of a reservoir take the distinct path on the right, soon to meet a crossing path. Here turn right downhill to meet edge of wood and cross stile and on through field to edge of housing estate. On the skyline will be seen the long line of the Clee Hills and nearer at hand the now familiar prospect of Bridgnorth's High Town.

Make your way through the housing estate; at end of the first road, Hazel View, bear right; at end of Oaklands turn right and at end of Elmhurst turn left. On reaching shops by telephone box turn right down St. Nicholas Road. At top of this road there is an excellent view of the town across the river. Descend a long series of steps to meet main road close to the Fox Inn and your starting point.

PLACES TO VISIT

MIDLAND MOTOR MUSEUM: Stanmore Hall. A458 east of Bridgnorth
    Collection of sports and racing cars and motor cycles. Gardens,
    Nature Trail etc., Camping Park for caravans and tents.
    Museum open daily except Dec 25. 10am-5pm.
    Tel: (0746) 761761.

*Stokesay Castle Gatehouse, from
the South Tower*

The Severn from High Rock, Bridgnorth

3: Severn Up

BASIC ROUTE DETAIL:	Bridgnorth, west bank of Severn up stream, Apley Bridge, Station House, Nordley, Astley Abbotts, Cross Lane Head, St Mary's Cottage, Cantern Brook, Bridgnorth.
MAPS:	1/25,000 SO69/79 (Pathfinder 911) 1/50,000 Landranger Sheet 138.
DISTANCE:	10½ miles approx.
CAR PARKING:	Low Town off A442 near Fox Inn.
TOILETS:	Opposite Fox Inn & by Market Hall Bridgnorth.
TOURIST INFORMATION:	The Library, Listley Street, Bridgnorth. Tel: 074 62 3358

From the Low Town car park turn left, then left again to cross the River Severn. Turn right into Cartway and after a few yards take the road on the right and follow Riverside. The sandstone cliffs on the left are providing a secure home for birds and sparrows are particularly active here. After a while the road narrows to become a track following the banks of the river, lined with willow trees.

Soon High Rock comes fully into view, the impressive cliff face with its greening of Scots pine contrasting with the red sandstone as it rises almost sheer from the river with only just enough room for the road to make a way between river and cliff.

After passing High Rock the path runs alongside the golf course and is soon passing the sandstone towers of Fort Pendlestone. From this low level route the walker has a different prospect of the high route explored in the last walk.

Long tailed tits are found in the trees that line the bank, perhaps visitors from the coniferous forest across the water. The River Worfe, the attractive river encountered in the last walk, makes its junction with the Severn on the opposite bank. At end of the golf course cross a stile and continue along the river bank. A feature of this walk is the view of the high wooded cliffs

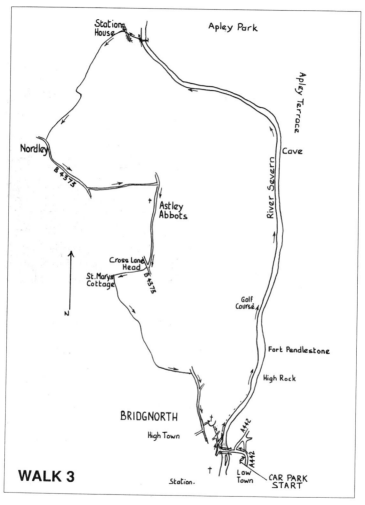

Station House

Apley Park

Apley Terrace

Nordley

B 4373

Cave

Astley Abbots

River Severn

Cross Lane Head

St. Marys Cottage

B 4373

Golf Course

N

Fort Pendlestone

High Rock

BRIDGNORTH

High Town

A442

A442

Station.

Low Town

CAR PARK START

WALK 3

that wall in the river on its east bank. The less than musical call of pheasants can be heard from the woods opposite.

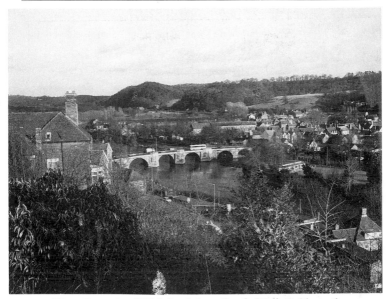

River Severn and High Rock from Castle Walk, Bridgnorth

Across the field to the left and running parallel is the low embankment of the now dismantled railway. On a winter's day in February we heard the melancholy sound of an owl calling across the river, not unlike the whistle of a locomotive, ghostly echoes of the past!

The fine but distant "black and white" buildings to the left are Severn Hall. Across the river more caves are seen cut into the cliffs near Winstone Cottage, beautifully sited high above the river. What a marvellous place this must be to live, particularly in the summer with a superb view of the valley of the Severn towards Bridgnorth.

The river curves slowly to the left with the high wooded cliffs of Apley Terrace across the water.

As the railway embankment, path and river come together, early spring walkers will find snowdrops and primroses in sheltered spots. You may also see something slightly more unusual: cormorants, a surprise since they are normally coastal residents, but now increasingly found around inland waters.

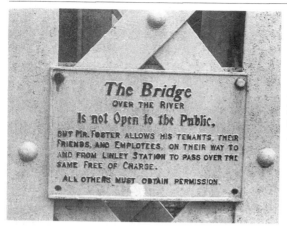

Free pass for friends - notice on the Apply Bridge

Stately *Apley Park comes into view, the home of the Wilmont family and later the Fosters. Soon a section of the river bank presents a problem; it has deteriorated to such an extent that even wellies would not guarantee a safe passage through the deep mud. A retreat must be made, by way of a stile, to the track of the old railway which can be followed until a gateway offers a return to the bank. (This is not an official right of way but local enquiries confirm that this is an accepted alternative).*

Ahead lies the handsome white-painted suspension bridge that linked the Apley Hall estate with the railway. It was built in 1905 by the then owner of Apley Hall, and is still maintained in excellent condition, a splendid ornament to the river scene. A notice on the bridge reads: "The bridge over the river is not open to the public but Mr Foster allows his tenants, their friends and his employees on their way to and from Linley station, to pass over the same, free of charge. All others must obtain permission."

After passing under the bridge turn left and pass the old station house.

Despite Mr Foster's generosity to his tenants, friends and employees, any such travellers today would have a disappointing wait. The last train ran in 1963 and the track was removed not long after. Indeed, but for the enterprise of the Severn Valley Railway Preservation Society the whole line would have been lost. Such is the success of their undertaking one can't help but wonder if one day they will be enabled to push the line north again from Bridgnorth.

Apley Hall was built by the Whitmore family early in the nineteenth century, in a superb position with commanding views of the river and the Shropshire landscape. The house passed on to the Fosters, who I understand were connected with the steel industry in Stourbridge. Recently it has seen service as a school and is now being renovated as a retirement home.

Cross the old railway track and continue ahead. After passing through a five barred gateway, the path is followed into a wood. After passing some cottages, continue forward ignoring a path to the left. The way is never very far from a little stream. Ignore first bridge on left by a broken gate. About 100 yards after passing under power lines, cross the stream by a little bridge and go forward over marshy ground to join a muddy bridleway uphill to meet a gate into wood. The path improves as height is gained.

When the edge of the wood is reached continue uphill with the wood to your left. When the trees fall back continue with a boundary fence to your left to meet the road by the Swan at Nordley, with its handsome inn sign.

Turn left and follow the road (B4373) for just over half a mile and turn left along a quiet lane when Colemore Green is signed. When a T-junction is reached, turn right to walk through the attractive little village with the splendid ecclesiastically alliterative name of Astley Abbots. It's a tiny village with well maintained black and white half timbered houses and a sandstone church. It still retains a Victorian post box, with the collection arrangements shown by the day rather than the hours.

Continue with the lane to reach the road, (B4373) at Cross Lane Head, with its signpost of the old type carrying the name of the village within a circle in addition to directions elsewhere. It always seemed a good idea to tell people where there were as well as where they were going. Other versions of this type of sign carried the grid reference of its location, not nearly so useful for the general traveller. Nor is it hard to see how this little settlement got its name.

Take the broad track opposite and follow for just over a quarter of a mile, just short of St Mary's Cottage. Here take footpath on the left, over waymarked stile to cross field. (Note the path seems to follow a different course to that shown on the map but the direction of travel is shown on waymarks on the stiles....at least on those that have not been vandalised). A second field is crossed diagonally right to bottom corner, cross stile and ditch and follow field boundary with Cantern Brook to your right.

At end of field meet a stile in a muddy corner and enter wood. Continue forward on rising and falling path with the brook sparkling and chattering to your right, another good habitat for birds. The path eventually descends to the brook to meet a bridge which is crossed. Here take the path on the left which climbs stepped path to continue forward with garden fences on your right.

When an open grassy area in front of a housing estate is reached, continue forward to meet path which runs along edge of wood to your left and again with garden fences to your right. A steeply wooded slope drops a hundred feet to the brook and among the plentiful population of birds blue tits and great tits seem to outnumber the others.

As the houses come to an end, the path descends with wire fence to your right. Soon a stream is crossed by a plank bridge, then up stepped path to continue forward to pass between a line of scots pines and shortly meet the road (B4373).

At the road turn right to enter Bridgnorth by Northgate, the only one remaining of the five that gave entrance, or forbade it, to the town.

The local museum is accommodated above the gate, with a thousand or so items reflecting something of the town's past. Admission is free.

By the Golden Lion there is a mounting block, a relic of the days when the inn provided sustenance and accommodation for travellers who arrived on horseback or by the stage coach.

After a short distance take the turning on the left which leads to St Leonard's church, with its handsome sandstone tower.

Whilst the church is no longer required for religious worship, it remains consecrated and is maintained by the Redundant Churches Fund. It was at this church the Royalists stored their powder kegs during the unhappy period of the Civil War, with disastrous results to the town and its people. This is a quiet spot reminiscent of the atmosphere of a cathedral close, if not quite on the same scale. The church door is likely to be found locked but a key can be obtained locally.

In the close, for that is what I am tempted to call it, is a little half timbered house with a sign which reads: "In this house lived the learned and eloquent Richard Baxter, 1640-1641". How rewarding to be remembered as learned and eloquent, especially after such a short residence, all too easy to spend a lifetime in one spot and fail to leave a mark!

Richard Baxter, was a Presbyterian minister, who after a short stay in Bridgnorth worked in the carpet town of Kidderminster, (Worcs). During the Civil War he became a chaplain with the Parliamentarian Army. His account of events and personal experience during this time has found its way into the histories of the period. He seems to have been an admirer of Cromwell, advocating his appointment as Lord Protector after the failure of the Commonwealth. Visitors to Kidderminster will find a handsome statue to Baxter outside the parish church.

Opposite the church are the galleried alms houses of the Palmer's Hospital Charity, built in 1687. They were "rebuilt and rendered more commodious, AD 1889, towards the cost of rebuilding, Mrs Colley, of Oldbury contributed £500.", in those days a very generous donation that would have carried the work forward a long way. The original inscription, now fading, reads:

"ADMDCLXXXVII, these alms houses for 10 poor widows of this towne were built and endowed by Francis Palmer, the rector of Sandy in the County of Bedford who had an affection to this place (?), his mother being buried in this church and was sister to Colonel Francis Billingsley, late of Abbots Astley (???), slain in this churchyard in the service of Charles the First."

A little beyond the Alms Houses is the narrow entrance to St Leonard's Steps, which, as a descent is made offers views over the river to Hermitage Hill and upstream to High Rock. On reaching the road continue downwards by Cartway passing the Prince Charles Inn and Bishop Percy's house with its elaborate patterning of its timbers. At foot of Cartway turn left to cross bridge and return to your starting point.

4: Bewdley and The Wyre Forest

BASIC ROUTE DETAIL:	Bewdley, east bank of Severn upstream, Dowles Brook, Wyre Forest - Knowles Mill, Park House, return by old railway track, Tanners Hill, Bewdley.
	NOTE: Part of this walk is on permissive rather than public footpaths, these are not open to the public on Christmas Day and New Year's Day.
MAPS:	1/25,000 SO67/77 (Pathfinder 952) 1/50,000 Landranger Sheet 138
DISTANCE:	8 miles approx.
CAR PARKING:	Dog Lane, Bewdley.
TOILETS:	Close to car park, Bewdley.
TOURIST INFORMATION:	Close to car park, Bewdley.

This walk trespasses across the Shropshire Border into neighbouring Hereford and Worcester, to follow a short stretch of the River Severn and explore the Wyre Forest.

There are not too many places where the motorist can arrive and park his car in the centre of the town and be off on his walking route in under a minute but this is the case with the Worcestershire town of Bewdley. Occupying an important position on the banks of the River Severn it has a satisfying long history with important connections with forestry, and the busy river traffic of the River Severn over many centuries.

This eight mile walk starts from the Dog Lane car park and follows the riverside then pursues the course of Dowles Brook deep into the Wyre Forest. The forest, which covers some six thousand acres, lies to the west of the Severn and there is ample opportunity to enjoy the rich wild life of the mixed woodland, which includes deer and a wide variety of birds.

From the car park turn left down Dog Lane to meet the river at Severnside North. Here turn left and follow a path along the bank. Across

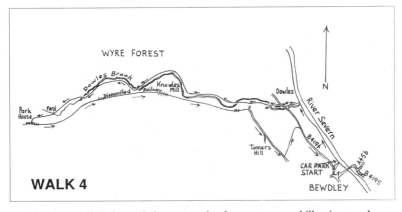

WYRE FOREST

WALK 4

BEWDLEY

the river, a little beyond the eastern bank, you may see billowing smoke from the locomotives of the Severn Valley Railway, which keeps close company with the river for much of its sixteen mile journey from Kidderminster to Bridgnorth.

The fast flowing Severn has long been in use as a highway for the movement of goods and Bewdley was one of a number of towns that prospered as a port, further aided by the generous supplies of local timber for boat building and charcoal burning and the early bridging of the river.

The riverside fringed with alders and pollarded willows is followed for about three quarters of a mile, until the tall brick pillars that once supported a railway bridge are seen ahead. Just before the pillars are reached, cross the footbridge over the Dowles Brook, turn left and in about three hundred yards reach the road, B4194 and turn right.

After a few yards pick up path on the left which is found just beyond the old bridge abutments. The path edges a nature reserve and soon swings left to cross the brook. To the right can be seen the topiaried gardens of Dowles Manor whilst to the left is the steep embankment of a now disused loop line of the Severn Valley Railway.

About a quarter of a mile after leaving the road a broad track is reached. Here turn right. After a short distance the path divides, take the right fork which again crosses the brook. The picturesque Oak Cottage is passed, it is a delightful woodland hideaway, set under the trees with blue tits, gold

Coracle on the River Severn at Bewdley. The town's lively museum holds coracle construction courses and a regatta every August

crest and blackcapped willow tit very active around the garden.

These woods, particularly along the streams, are rich in bird life, wagtails and dippers are to be seen. At the time of our last visit we heard that a heron had been fishing at the same spot on the Dowles Brook every day for weeks. The yaffling cry of the green wood-pecker is almost certain to be heard and so will the harsh call of the jay. This colourful bird is an acorn eater and like the squirrel stores acorns for winter food. Spring should be a particularly rewarding time for the birdwatcher, with the returning migratory birds likely to be more visible before being lost in the foliage of summer. A tawny owl may be heard, or a fleeting glimpse of a kingfisher caught as it flashes along the stream.

It is not only birds that will be seen and heard, the forest is home to a number of deer (four hundred has been suggested) and even if you miss seeing them, their slotted tracks in softer ground will confirm their presence. Squirrels abound, and despite efforts to keep them in check feral mink are thriving and no doubt taking their toll of fish and birds eggs. Until recently crayfish could be found in the cool clear waters of the brook, but they have now been wiped out by a fungal infection.

Our route passes Knowles Mill, it dates from at least 1757 and had a long working life, being in service up to the beginning of this century. It was purchased by the Cadbury family in the 1930's and presented to the National Trust. The nearby cottage is much older and may have already passed its four hundredth birthday, certainly there is a written record of it in 1661.

The walker may have seen a "Danger - Adders" notice posted by the Nature Conservancy Council. Local naturalists Sylvia Sheldon and Chris Bradley have been making a careful study of the snakes in the forest for several years. A count of adult adders in 1988 produced a tally of 205 over the entire Wyre Forest area. They think that perhaps there ought to be "Danger - People" notice for the adder population. The snakes are quick to disappear when danger threatens and more often than not are on their way well before you have a chance to see them.

Do not cross the brook at Knowles Mill but continue still with the stream to your left. Shortly after passing Coopers Mill Youth Centre the track turns left and crosses a stream. Once over the bridge turn sharp right and follow line of stream. Soon the path divides, ignore left junction and go forward on the rising path looking down upon the brook. About half a mile after the last crossing of the brook the path again returns to the other bank and swings left. After a short distance a forest road is reached, turn left along this and in about a quarter of a mile reach a ford. A few paces to the right you can cross dry shod by way of the footbridge.

The track now runs away from the river, climbing towards Park House and lined with elegant silver birches and young oaks. As Park House is reached, the line of the old railway is met running east to west. Turn left along this and follow for nearly two miles. The walker alternates between delightful prospects of the brook winding through the forest two hundred feet below on one hand, being lost to the world in sheltered cuttings, and on the other side of the track catch glimpses of steep tree clad clefts with tiny streams glistening in the gullies.

Winter walking in the Wyre Forest

As a gate just beyond a bridge is reached a track leads off to Lodge Hill Farm; note the bat boxes on the trees to the left. Beyond the bridge the track is metalled: continue with this until a T-junction is made with a narrow lane. Here turn right and follow it uphill between hedges with improving views.

When a road junction is met, ignore Hop Pole Lane on the right and continue forward. At the summit houses are met. Here take the path signed off to the left. This descends over several fields, offering views of the Severn and the surrounding wooded hillsides. When metalled track is reached by a house, turn right and meet the road (B4194).

Turn right along the road, making your way back to Bewdley; your starting point in Dog Lane is found in just over quarter of a mile.

(Authors acknowledgements: I am indebted to local naturalists Sylvia Sheldon and Chris Bradley for some of the information in this chapter.)

PLACES TO VISIT

BEWDLEY MUSEUM: Load Street. Open March-November.
Mon-Sat inc: Bank Holidays. 10am-5.30pm.
Sundays 2-5.30pm.

BEWDLEY TOWN TRAIL: Explore Bewdley with aid of the Town trail leaflet, available from Information Centre.

WEST MIDLAND SAFARI PARK: Spring Grove, Bewdley.

Tel: 0299 402114

WYRE FOREST CENTRE: Callow Hill. On the A456 west of Bewdley.
Forest trail leaflet available.

WYRE FOREST WALKING: As above but there are car parks also off B4194, north-west of Bewdley.

5: The Wrekin Giants

BASIC ROUTE:	Forest Glen, south-eastern flank of The Wrekin return over Little Hill and summit.
MAPS:	1/25,000 Pathfinder 890 (SJ60/70)
DISTANCE:	5 miles approx.
TOURIST INFORMATION:	The Toll House, Ironbridge. Tel: 095245 2753.
CAR PARKING:	Off road by Forest Glen about 1½ miles north of Little Wenlock.
TOILETS:	At eastern foot of The Wrekin.

The Wrekin, 1335 feet, rises sharply from the surrounding countryside. At almost any weekend the car parking spaces are in full use as a fair number of people take a walk over The Wrekin; to the summit and back. Its popularity is related to the close proximity of Telford New Town and the tourist area of Ironbridge, coupled with its excellence as a viewpoint. Most of these visitors take the direct approach from the east and few of them find their way beyond the summit. Whilst it unquestionably offers rewarding views for a modest effort, it is not the best approach, the ascent from the west being more visually satisfying, with the Shropshire scenery gradually unrolling as the walk develops.

Take the steadily rising broad track opposite the Forest Glen, ignoring all paths to the right. Through the trees will be seen the steep face of the quarry by the car park, where the climbers practice their sport.

A sharp elbow in the track marks a change in direction and a quarter of a mile from this the path turns sharp right for the direct approach to the summit. Resist this temptation and continue forward on a good track through the wood, immediately passing the collapsed remains of a building on your left. The path is muddy in places, encouraged by slow trickles of water out of the steeply falling hillside. Birch and oak rise above the bracken and bramble on the floor of the forest. Gaps in the trees provide windows onto hills whose shapes have been re-sculptured by man's quest for their stone treasure.

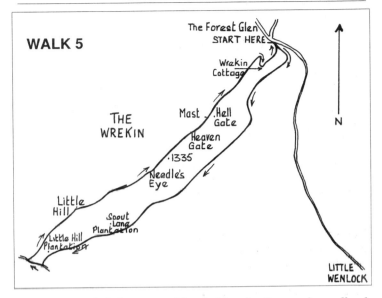

The Forest Glen
START HERE

Wrekin
Cottage

THE
WREKIN

Mast. .Hell
Gate

Heaven
Gate

·1335

Needle's
Eye

Little
Hill

Spout
Lane
Plantation

Little Hill
Plantation

N

LITTLE
WENLOCK

These wooded slopes provide a habitat for the usual woodland birds and nuthatch are found throughout the year. This small bird, about five and half inches, may be seen giddily descending a tree head first. Other regulars are the green woodpecker and great spotted woodpecker, both of whom nest in holes bored into tree trunks, at least one such nesting site is passed along the way. There are badgers, foxes and some seldom seen deer, escapees from the National Trust's Attingham Park.

Away to the left will be seen plumes of steam rising from the Buildwas Power Station, like huge pots on the hob about to boil over, giving modern credence to the story of the Wrekin giants. As the path advances there are glimpses of the Stretton Hills to the west.

When the path divides, ignore left fork to the Shropshire County Scout Camp and go forward through Spout Lane and Little Hill Plantations to reach the road. Here turn right and after two hundred yards re-enter wood by path on the right signed with the buzzard waymark of the Shropshire Way.

The path rises steadily through the conifers. Ignore all turnings to left and right. After a broad track is crossed the path steepens to climb to the summit of Little Hill. The hillside has been cleared and recently replanted, giving excellent views from this comparatively modest height, crowned with a small clutch of Scots pines.

From Little Hill, the digitalis lined path dips, gathering strength for the ascent through the trees to The Wrekin summit. The climb is as steep as many a mountain, and increasingly frequent pauses for breath give a tunnel's eye backward view thorough an avenue of trees to the Stretton Hills.

At last the first view point at the western end of The Wrekin is reached. Here the walker is on top of the world, with the wind roaring in from the west battering the trees and threatening to dislodge him from his rocky perch. Beneath is the familiar pattern of pasture and plough divided by a network of hedgerows, one of the hallmarks of the English landscape. The tall cooling towers indicate the approach to Ironbridge, beyond the shapely towers the wooded hills rise sharply to make the western wall of the gorge. In the distance a great semi-circle of hills, Clee Hills, Long Mynd and the other Stretton heights. In the flat land ahead the Severn's meandering passage through the pastures is clearly seen, a silvered gleam quite unlike the muddy brown so often seen at closer quarters, before it is funnelled through the gorge.

In the far distance at the outer edge of the circle the grey blue smudge where sky and hills meet mingle into one and it is difficult to discern the difference between cloud and solid earth. Can you really see Snowdon on a clear day? It is a great place to watch the weather. On a fine day observe the gentle progress of high white clouds of summer casting their cooling shadows upon the fields below. In winter, to willingly endure the wind's blast as the storm clouds come scudding across the Welsh borders, racing over the Long Mynd and Caer Caradoc, their heavy burden of snow pressed forward by an angry wind. In autumn to watch the sun shafting through the clouds, spot lighting varying features, a single farmhouse, the plumes of steam rising from the cooling towers, the crown of a distant hill, or its warming light bringing greater depths of colour to the trees and the browning of the bracken. All scenes from the theatre of the sky, adding to the richness of the landscape

Under The Wrekin

that makes all the year round walking such a pleasure come rain,
shine, or snow.

    *Just short of the summit a little path passes under the volcanic rocks that
had their fiery creation six hundred million years ago, a path that edges the*

49

steeply falling hillside.

The Needle's Eye, a cleft rock which legend says was split in twain at the instant of the crucifixion. How the dwellers here on the old hill top camp could possibly have known of the events in The Holy Land is never explained. Another story associated with the rock, (and there are similar stories elsewhere) that a young lady taking the narrow passage through the eye was obliged to give her escort a kiss on emerging on the other side. Those thoughtless enough to look back would pay the penalty of never marrying.

The story of how The Wrekin was formed is similar to ones related about other isolated hills. A giant (or the devil) is on his way with a great shovelful of earth to take his revenge on a nearby town - in this case, Shrewsbury. He meets a cobbler with a sackful of shoes which he has collected for repair. The giant asks the cobbler the way, and the wily cobbler tells him that he has already worn out all the shoes in the bag trying to find the way. The frustrated giant then dumps the earth, abandoning his intention to damn the Severn with a view to flooding Shrewsbury. Thus we have The Wrekin.

Other versions of the story involve a fight between two giants who were building a home on The Wrekin. They fell out over the use of a shared spade, during the course of a violent argument the spade split the rock we now call the Needle's Eye.....there's more, but enough is enough of tall stories!

The broad track over the summit passes through the western gate of the hill fort to arrive at the topograph presented by the Wellington Rotary Club to commemorate the Queen's Silver Jubilee in 1977.

The pointer answers all those questions about distant landmarks. To the west, Caer Caradoc $12^{1}/_{2}$ miles; Pole Bank Long Mynd, 16 miles; Devil's Chair on the Stiperstones, $17^{1}/_{2}$ miles. Towards the north, the world's largest doric column honours Rowland Hill, Shrewsbury's famous general. To the north west Snowdon, 71 miles; Berwyn Mountains, 37 miles. To the south the Malvern Hills, 40 miles, and more splendid walking with Clee Hill and Wenlock Edge 8 miles away, just to the west of south.

The biblical connection suggested by the Needle's Eye, is extended as the walker continues over the summit to pass through Heaven's Gate to descend a little (of course) before passing through Hell Gate. There is a television mast tucked under the edge of the hill fort, a modern addition to the ancient home of the Cornovii.

There is a firing range on the north of the hill, and the path is edged with a number of warning notices and flags. As height is lost the paths divide, take path on right. Cross a broad track, pass Wrekin Cottage to your right and continue with the broad track which winds steadily downhill to return to your starting point.

PLACES TO VISIT

ATTINGHAM PARK: NT Property built for Lord Berwick in 1785.
Fine state rooms. Deer park.
Open 25 March to end Sept Sat to Wed 2.00-5.30pm.
Bank Hol Mons 11.30am-5.30pm.

Oct Sat & Sun 2.00-5.30pm.

BENTHALL HALL: Broseley. 16th cent house and garden.
Easter Sun to end Sept. Tues, Wed, Sun and Bank Hol Mons 2.00-6.00pm.

VIROCONIUM: Roman town at Wroxeter with small museum.

6: Wenlock Edge and The Desperate Rider

BASIC ROUTE:	Much Wenlock, Blakeway Hollow, Majors Leap, Blakeway Coppice, Harley Wood, Stokes Barn.
MAPS:	1/25,000. This section of the Edge inconveniently spreads over 3 sheets. SO49/59: SO69/79 (Pathfinder 911) Pathfinder 890 (SJ60/70).
DISTANCE:	5¹/₂ miles approx.
CAR PARKING:	NT car park off B4371 or Much Wenlock.
TOILETS:	Much Wenlock car park.
TOURIST INFORMATION:	Guildhall, Much Wenlock.

When the walker comes to Wenlock Edge he is in Houseman Country, so evocatively recalled in his "A Shropshire Lad", published in 1896. Houseman writes of the hills, the little towns and the rivers which we are exploring and as Elgar walked the Malvern Hills and found the inspiration for some of his great music, surely Houseman found the magic of his words upon The Wrekin, along the Edge, or reflected in the silvered waters of Severn, Teme or Corve.

Wenlock Edge, as narrow as its name suggests, runs for some fifteen miles between Much Wenlock and Craven Arms, its limestone spine the legacy of the time, hundreds of millions of years ago, when warm tropical seas washed over this countryside. The long legged and stout hearted may be tempted to walk the Edge, end to end. Subject to appropriate transport or accommodation being arranged it is both a practical and appealing prospect. In this connection YHA members will be aware of the hostel at Wilderhope Manor. Small parties who are able to station a car at either end have quickly solved the problem, but for walkers who prefer shorter expeditions or a more leisurely exploration I have suggested three round walks by way of an introduction. The possibility of merging parts of these walks to provide variations will not escape the reader.

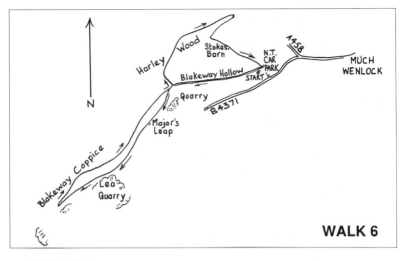

WALK 6

THE WALK

*Leave the National Trust car park by the stepped path to join Blakeway
Hollow. Here turn left to follow this wide track, the relic of an old road,
rising steadily with improving views. From time to time remains of old
limestone kilns will be seen. These kilns were used to reduce the stone to
agriculturally usable lime. The way is edged by now overgrown drystone
walls, so often an indicator of good walking country.*

*A twin ridge is seen to the left, its green banks rising swiftly from the
scoop of the dale, while to the north east the tree clad Wrekin imposes its
presence upon the scene.*

*As the summit of the lane is reached the path divides, take the left fork
which passes through a six barred gate. Soon on the left a white waymarked
sign points the direction of Major's Leap. This path follows the inside edge
of the wood, with ramson, that pungent flower of the woodland, beginning
to show through in spring. Shortly a stepped path carries the walker a little
higher to follow a narrow path with steep slopes to the right and glimpses
of the landscape through the trees, somewhat more visible in winter than
when summer leaf jealously hides it from view. A bridle path parallels our
way on the outer edge of the wood and above the quarries. From here the
stratified layers of stone are clearly seen, composed of the skeletons of*

countless billions of sea creatures, whose fossilized remains continue to be found.

Ahead Brown Clee Hill is seen, its winter's powdering of snow giving it a resemblance to a Christmas pudding topped with white sauce, a radio mast doing duty as a holly sprig, completing this fanciful illusion.

Major's Leap is reached in half a mile from the signpost.

It was here, the story goes, that Major Smallman of Wilderhope Manor, made a legendary escape. During the Civil War, as a Royalist he found himself the fox in a life or death pursuit; the pack that followed him were the supporters of the Parliamentary cause. The hunters were gaining fast upon him and the cliff-like slopes of Wenlock Edge were before him. Escape seemed quite impossible, but he urged his mount forward into one last death-defying leap off the high edge. Incredibly, although his horse was killed beneath him, the Major survived to limp away, borrow another horse and make fully good his escape!

Wintry day on Major's Leap, Wenlock Edge

The "leap" is marked by a small seat. Here the trees fall back a little allowing views to the Long Mynd and the Stretton Hills. An excellent place to pause and enjoy the landscape.

The quarries have made substantial inroads and here the edge is perhaps not too far from having disappeared altogether; a reminder of the fragile environment in which we live.

From Major's Leap continue forward on the outside edge of the wood; beech, ash and some Scots pine.

Ahead Brown Clee Hill achieves increasing prominence until the eyes and ears are distracted by the rattle of machinery and the roar of dumper trucks as the main quarry buildings are neared. When the walker draws level with these buildings, albeit situated beneath him on the quarry floor, the path comes to an abrupt end. At this point take the path signed off to the right to Presthope.

Descend the hillside on a narrow path to reach a broad track. The route to the left will eventually lead to a further car park at Presthope, ignore this and turn right to return on a parallel course signposted to Much Wenlock, 2 miles.

At the time of writing winter forestry operations have turned the track to the consistency of liquid cement. Soon a couple of seats placed with a view forward to Blakeway Farm and the dale beyond allows the opportunity for comfortable refreshment.

When the path divides, ignore left fork, and continue forward, soon to pass under Major's Leap, where Smallman, the Evil Knevil of his day made his prodigious jump.

Continue forward ignoring the small stepped path on the right that would return you to the Leap. As the edge of the wood is reached the outward route is joined for a few yards. Just beyond the gate take a path on left signed to Harley Bank. A wide path that curves to the right to descend through the trees giving occasional glimpses of the long line of the Edge running off to the west.

When the path divides ignore turn to the right and continue until a gateway is reached at the edge of the wood which gives onto a broad track. Here The Wrekin is seen boldly ahead. Do not join the parallel track on the left but continue forward on the track which rises through a conifer plantation.

The Jenny Wind Incline which carried limestone to the kilns crosses the track, and the Shrewsbury road is seen through the cleared ground that accommodated its passage. Continue forward with a stand of tall and slender birch trees to the left and The Wrekin showing through the lattice work of their trailing twigs.

Soon the grey waymarked route is rejoined to continue forward with the Shrewsbury Road again seen at the foot of a steep bank. At the top of the rise, turn right, signed Much Wenlock, ¾ mile. The bank on the right is sheltered, catching the sun for most of the day, the primroses flower early here, a welcome sign of spring for the walker.

The path climbs steadily, passing a badger's sett and giving improving views over the plain towards Shrewsbury and to the great bulk of The Wrekin when cleared spaces allow.

The path dips a little before climbing a stepped path. Just beyond the top of the steps, take the path signed Much Wenlock to pass through a gate and follow the left hand edge of a field towards the limestone buildings at Stokes Barn with its impressively large doors. The evidence of former quarrying in the fields suggests the possibility that the buildings were constructed from materials found on site.

Just beyond the house swing off to the right to meet a waymark post. A short field is crossed to pass through a gate and take descending path over a field which leads to a stile. Here turn left into Blakeway Hollow and after a few steps turn right over stile to return to the car park.

PLACES TO VISIT

MUCH WENLOCK

MUSEUM Weekdays 10.30am-1.00pm. 2.00-5.00pm.
Sundays June-Aug at same times.

GUILDHALL April to Sept. Weekdays except when court sits - first
Thursday in month - 11.00am-12.30pm and 2.30-5.00pm
Sundays 2.00-5.00pm

PRIORY RUINS 15th March to 15th Oct.
Weekdays 9.30am-6.30pm Sundays 2.00-6.30pm
Mid Oct to Mid March
Weekdays 9.30am-4.00pmSundays 2.00-4.00pm

7: Ippikin's Rock and Spring Lamb

BASIC ROUTE:	Presthope - Ippikin's Rock - Easthope Wood
	Easthope - Natal Coppice -
	Dove Plantation Presthope.
MAPS:	1/25,000 SO49/59
	1/50,000 Landranger 137
DISTANCE:	5 miles approx.
CAR PARKING:	NT car park, Presthope B4371 SW of Much Wenlock.
TOILETS:	Much Wenlock.
TOURIST INFORMATION:	Guildhall. Much Wenlock.

The walk starts from the National Trust car park on the B4371 about 3 miles south west of Much Wenlock.

From the car park take the wide, signposted bridleway which descends through the woods, passing some venerable yew trees. After about a hundred yards the path divides, here turn left. This is something of a wild flower walk; in spring primroses edge the track and wood anemones, another herald of spring, are seen in profusion. At the foot of the hill, turn left along a lane which runs along the edge of the wood to reach and cross the Hughley road.

Take the path opposite to climb through the woods; a glance back will reveal the great bulk of The Wrekin. Another favourite spring flower, the little violet, is found just off the path and an occasional celandine. After about 150 yards of a frankly disagreeably muddy path, a stile gives onto the broad track of an old railway. Here turn right and then immediately left to take the uphill path signed to Ippikin's Rock. The woodlands have an undercover of wild flowers, some rather distant from the path, but nevertheless seen brightly through the trees.

The path rises and falls, but ignore all turnings, maintaining your direction by reference to the green arrowed waymarks until Ippikin's Rock is signed by a stout post. A short uphill pitch lined with ramsons.

Having walked quietly and alone through the woods it is a minor

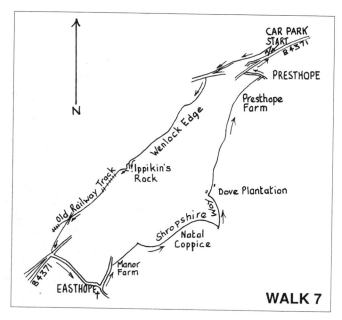

WALK 7

surprise to find the summit already occupied. Ippikin's Rock is close to the road and the Wenlock Edge Inn and in consequence is a stopping place on the tourist route. First the view, then the legend. The views that have so far been denied to the walker are now revealed as he stands on the edge of this rocky observation post, looking beyond the steeply falling, tree covered Edge to the green dale, still well hedged and with a haphazzard scatter of farms. The Stretton Hills fill the left horizon while away to the right The Wrekin will be seen - a sweeping view, not overly dramatic, but the cliché "green and pleasant land" springs to the mind.

The village to the north is Hughley which has achieved a perverse sort of fame owing to Houseman's poetic licence in conveniently amending the architecture of its church: he changed its tower to steeple in order to rhyme with people! Actually, he gets the best of both worlds by calling it a tower a few lines on.

On the edge - enjoying the view from Ippikin's Rock, Wenlock Edge

Ippikin cannot be cast in the same mould as the dashing Major Smallman, in fact, he appears to have been no more than a common criminal. Legend has it that he was the leader of a band of thieves who hid themselves and their ill-gotten gains in a cave beneath the rock. Justice seems to have triumphed in the end when a fall of rock sealed the cave and brought a not undeserved conclusion to their nefarious careers.

Having enjoyed the view, and possibly the hospitality of the Inn, retrace your steps to your original path just below the rock. Here turn left and after a short distance make a junction (no pun intended) with the old railway track and turn left with it.

Just after crossing a bridge over a lane the walker encounters a 'Private Woods - Please Do Not Trespass' sign. Here the railway track must be left. Take the lane uphill to meet and cross the B4371, taking the road opposite signed to Easthope. Brown Clee Hill shows up a little mistily and violets

Hughley Church

and wood anemones are found on the banks of the lane.

Easthope is a small, peaceful village lying beneath the Edge, with a mix of half timbered and stone buildings. It is a delightful place to be in the spring with lambing in full swing with the farmyards turned into maternity wards for the new arrivals.

The young lambs are full of fun and are soon on their feet and out in the fields, running pell mell in little groups, or playing king of the castle on any little mound that will serve the purpose. Sheep cover the opposite hillside, looking like a distant fleet of sailing ships upon a sea of green. Think not of mint sauce at a time like this.

From the village take the lane signed to Much Wenlock and after three hundred yards take the wide track on the right to make a rather circuitous return to Presthope on waymarked paths that form part of the Shropshire Way.

At end of the first field pass through a metal gateway as the path bears right and head to a gateway opposite which carries the buzzard waymark. Once through the gate bear half left across the field with Natal Coppice to your right. An arrow on a telegraph post points the way, the path following the outside edge of the coppice. As the coppice falls back head for the opposite field boundary to cross a stile by an ancient oak in a corner of the field. Go forward on a path closed in by wooded hedges to emerge into an open field. Here turn left to follow the field edge down a slope towards Dove Plantation. A stile is crossed to follow the short edge of the Plantation to a further stile and gate reached in about a hundred yards.

Once over the stile go forward for a short distance with a hedge on your left. Just before a pond is reached, a waymark on an old stump by a metal gate directs you right, to cross a field to pass a second pond on your right, then to meet and follow a field edge with a fence on your left. Shortly after passing a gateway (do not go through) join the hedged track ahead, which whilst once wide enough for farm carts is now somewhat obstructed by brambles and the like.

After emerging from a mild battle with the forces of nature, the path heads diagonally, roughly north-east to a metal gate and to join a track. After a short distance this merges with a quarry road, but the path soon goes forward (on right) to join the road. Here turn left to ascend to the B4371.

Turn right at the junction, passing the English China Clay's quarry works with its great stacks of neatly cut stone ready for delivery. After a short distance the car park which was the starting point of this walk is seen ahead.

8: Hope Dale and The Edge

BASIC ROUTE:	Easthope, Lutwyche, Pilgrim's Lane, The Edge, Wilderhope, Lower Stanway, Hopes Cross, Stanway Coppice, Wrensnest, Pilgrim Cottage, Easthope.
MAPS:	1/25,000 SO49/59
	1/50,000 137
DISTANCE:	9 miles approx.
CAR PARKING:	see text.
TOURIST INFORMATION:	Guildhall, Much Wenlock.

This is the last of the Wenlock Edge walks scheduled for this book, although it will be clear from a study of the map there is further good walking in the area. In this connection attention is drawn to the picnic site further along the Edge between Harton and Upper Westhope which is in the centre of a long stretch of footpath which follows the Edge.

Car parking is a little awkward for this walk since there is nowhere in Easthope where you can responsibly leave a car and resort has to be made to one of the lay-bys on the B4371 on the Edge. The nearest is about 500 yards south-west of the Lushcott/Easthope crossing, very small but will accommodate perhaps two cars.

From the suggested lay-by make your way back to the cross-roads and turn right, downhill towards Easthope. After about three hundred yards take the path on the right through a metal gate to follow a broad track with a farm to your left. After passing a handsome house on left, pass through an iron gate and follow waymarked direction heading for Lutwyche Hall seen ahead. The route follows an indistinct track to the right of a broken line of trees. When a further gate is seen ignore this and continue forward with a wire fence to your right.

As a large dutch barn is reached, pass through a metal gate which carries a yellow arrow and the buzzard sign of the Shropshire Way and turn immediately left on a broad track to pass Lutwyche Hall on your right.

It is a handsome building but one that suffered a recent tragedy.

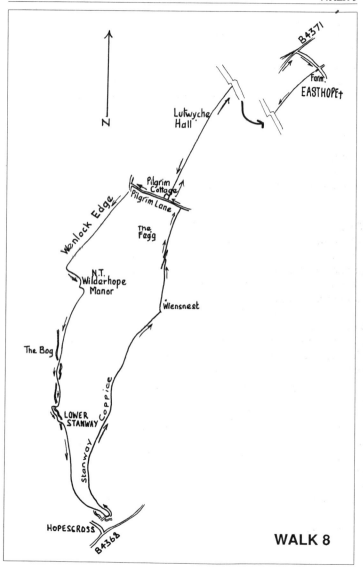

B4371

Farm.
EASTHOPE†

Lutwyche
Hall

Pilgrim
Cottage

Pilgrim Lane

Wenlock Edge

The
Fegg

N.T.
Wilderhope
Manor

Wlensnest

The Bog

Stanway Coppice

LOWER
STANWAY

HOPESCROSS

B4368

WALK 8

Walker on The Shropshire Way,
passing Lutwyche Hall, Wenlock Edge

Seven years had been spent on restoration work to the east wing
when early in 1989 a fire destroyed the roof and much of the effort
which had been put into the conservation of the wing. The Hall is in

The Iron Bridge, Ironbridge

Walkers on the Long Mynd

Heather in flower on Pole Bank, Long Mynd

the best tradition of the English Country House, enhancing the beautiful setting in which it was built. Mellowed brick towers rise either side of the south entrance with high mullioned windows topped with balconies balancing the towers. The house looks out across Hope Dale to the heights of the Mogg Forest, the highest point of which accommodates an old hill fort.

From the Hall there is a good stretch of walking along a broad straight track to reach Pilgrim's Cottage.

It is clearly an old building and should have a story attached to its name. Locally it is believed to be associated with another row of cottages on the Edge, now gone, whose occupants together with those of Pilgrim Cottage took passage on the Mayflower to the New World in search of the religious freedom denied them in their home country.

At the cottage turn right up a narrow lane and continue to the wood at the top. Here turn left with the dark recesses of the wood on your right. In spring, wood anemones, bluebells and primroses are to be found with other wild flowers to follow in season.

After a short distance a five barred gate is met and from hereon the path follows the outside edge of the wood with views opening up here and there through the gaps in the trees to give a sight across Ape Dale and with the lumps and bumps of the Stretton Hills forward right. The little settlement of Longville in the Dale is seen to the right.

Three fields are crossed along the wood edge until a covered reservoir topped by a small weather vane is seen. Here turn left and head down hill towards Wilderhope Manor. The Manor, which had hitherto been out of sight, soon comes into view with its tall chimneys and projecting rounded stair well, a patina of dignified age apparent upon its lichen roof and mellowed stone walls.

The Manor, owned by the National Trust, is a Youth Hostel, and whilst now furnished to fulfil that function is nevertheless open to the public on two afternoons a week. (detail end of chapter) This was the home of the gallant Major Smallman, an officer in the Royalist Army who made his death-defying leap further up Wenlock Edge and whose story has already been related. It is a handsome house dating from the sixteenth century and something of its history can be learned from the board on one of the outbuildings. One of the interesting features is a great rack above the fireplace in the dining hall which once held thirteen bows; now only five arrows remain of this armament store.

From the Manor cross the waymarked stile, with 'Corve Dale' incised into its timbers, to continue on the Shropshire Way to Lower Stanway and Hopes Cross as follows.

Follow the broad track to pass farm buildings and at a division of paths, indicated by two stiles, take the left choice - still with the broad track. The path curves with the boundary hedge on your right to pass a clump of trees in an area known as The Bog. At the end of the wood cross a plank bridge and turn half left to follow a wire fence on the left with a stream beyond. At the field corner, cross a waymarked stile and go immediately left to cross a plank bridge, then right to follow the stream edge. Jump a few small ditches, then a stile gives onto a lane at Lower Stanway.

Turn right over bridge and in a few paces turn left over a stile to follow the stream on your left. At end of a short field a further stile is crossed, then over a small stone bridge, turning right to follow the stream.

Continue with the path through the fields, resisting all temptations to cross the stream, however inviting the little bridges may seem. Eventually Brown Clee Hill is seen ahead making the southern backcloth to the scene. As Hopes Cross is neared a small row of cottages is seen on your left, cross the track which leads to them and go forward to a waymarked stile and through the remains of an old orchard. After a short distance swing left through a gap in the hedge.

We now start the return leg of the walk, following the great curve of the Stanway Coppice which rides the long ridge above Corve Dale.

Make your way uphill keeping to the outside of the coppice from which the heady scent of bluebells escapes in the spring and with glimpses through the trees down to the valley along which you have just travelled. At end of the first large field, pass through a metal gateway and continue on a broad track passing an old quarry, now very obviously a dumping ground for the unwanted. As height is gained the tips of the Stretton Hills are seen gradually gaining prominence.

Beyond the summit the wood falls away, but continue forward along the line of the hedge to meet the bottom edge of the plantation. Here pass through gate on your left and head diagonally right over field to meet and pass through gateway by a giant ash tree. This is a good spot for a photograph looking down the valley towards the distant Fegg farm. Beyond the gate to the right is Wrensnest delightfully, if remotely situated, and

Wilderhope Manor - home of the galloping Major Smallman

now unhappily in an advanced state of ruin . . . clearly the birds have flown.

Follow the edge of field with boundary to your right. As the path drops steadily downhill, Wilderhope Manor can be seen away to the left, set under the wooded Edge. Cross a stile but ignore direction arrow and once over a plank bridge set off diagonally half-right to the opposite corner of the field with a farm seen ahead. Cross a ditch and pass through gate to turn right and follow the edge of field with ditch, or stream if you prefer to afford it a little dignity, on your right.

At the end of the field the ditch is crossed. Pass through a metal gateway and continue forward to meet the edge of a plantation and join Pilgrims Lane as it runs towards Mogg Forest.

Turn left along the lane and on reaching Pilgrims' Cottage turn right to retrace your steps towards Easthope.

The little church at Easthope with its squat tower is seen ahead on the return. It has had something of a chequered history. It has the distinction of still retaining the hour glass which used to measure the length if not the value of the parson's sermon. It is housed in a wooden case dated 1662, bearing the initials of SS: Samuel Steadman.

Whether it was his idea to measure his performance, making sure he gave full measure, or whether it was there at the suggestion of his long suffering flock who felt that an hour was quite long enough thank you does not transpire. (When I visited the church early in 1989 it was missing; only a temporary absence I hope.)

The church yard contains the tombs of two monks of Wenlock Abbey who murdered each other during a drunken fight at the manor house. An earlier incumbent murdered his Patron, John Esthope, in 1333 and his ghost is reputed to have haunted the churchyard ever since. Church was never like this in my young day, and perhaps you should be cautious about speaking to any unfashionably dressed strangers you may encounter in this area, especially if cowled or cloaked. It therefore comes as no surprise that somehow the building was burnt down in 1928, cause unknown, speculation invited.

PLACES TO VISIT

WILDERHOPE MANOR: Wednesday and Sunday afternoons
           end of March to end of September 2.00-4.30pm.
           October-March Sats 2.00-4.30pm.

9: The Stiperstones

BASIC ROUTE	Cranberry Rocks along ridge to Shepherd's Rock, Perkins Beach, Stiperstones Village, Snailbeach (edge of) Crows Nest, Castle Ring Fort, Blakemoor Flat, Old Tips, Shepherd's Rock, Gattan Plantation.
MAPS:	1/25000 Sheets SJ20/30 and Pathfinder 909 (SO29/39) 1/50000 Landranger Sheets 126 and 137.
DISTANCE:	7 miles approx.
TOURIST INFORMATION:	Shropshire Hills Info Centre, Church St., Church Stretton. Tel: 722535. (If closed library next door)
CAR PARKING:	Two miles north west of Bridges on right of road under eastern side of Cranberry Rocks. If further exploration of the area is undertaken, note two large car parks beyond ridge on same road.

The Stiperstones is a three mile long ridge bisected by a narrow winding road. The southern half is mainly forested but the northern section is high bare moorland rising to 1760 feet, with rocky outcrops adding drama to the landscape. It forms part of a National Nature Reserve covering some 1100 acres and information boards at a number of points have maps showing the main paths and other information. More detailed background is also to be found on the western side of the hill in the area known as The Bog, once a small mining community, from which further expeditions can be started.

It is a remote area, not far from the Welsh border, as will be noted from the map titles of the 1/25000 Sheets, Montgomery and Welshpool. Some directions may be helpful to the motorist in finding the starting point of the walk. Leave the A49 at Church Stretton and after passing through the town centre take Burway Road which makes a spectacular climb high above the Carding Mill Valley to the top of the Long Mynd. When the road divides take the

69

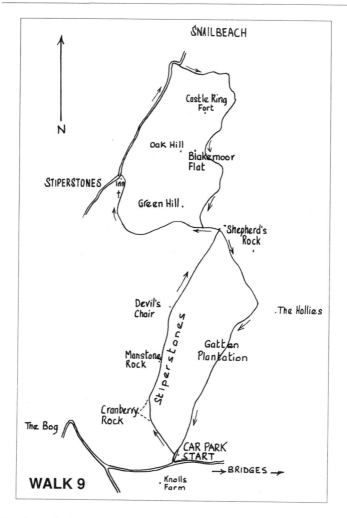

SNAILBEACH

Castle Ring Fort

Oak Hill

Blakemoor Flat

STIPERSTONES   Inn

Green Hill.

Shepherd's Rock

Devil's Chair

The Hollies

Stiperstones

Manstone Rock

Gatten Plantation

Cranberry Rock

The Bog

CAR PARK START

BRIDGES →

WALK 9

Knolls Farm

right branch signed to Ratlinghope and an equally exciting descent if you have only just learned to drive, thence to Bridges and on to the eastern edge of the Stiperstones ridge where a large car park is

*Walkers on
Cranberry Rocks.
The Stiperstones*

found.....(this is marked on the 1/50000 map).

*From the car park head up the wide grassy track and as height is gained
take the path diagonally left to visit Cranberry Rocks, one of a series of rocky
outcrops, reminiscent of the Dartmoor tors, which erupt spine like along
the ridge, adding greatly to the dramatic quality of the landscape.*

*The upper slopes of the ridge are heather covered and the going rough in
places with shattered quartz like rock littering the peaty way over the tops.
A rock that glints in the sun setting needle sharp points of light winking
at your feet. A mild scramble will take the walker to the top of the rocks to
survey the view.*

To the west is Wales, Corndon Hill large on the skyline is actually
across the border in Powys. Behind it Offa's Dyke makes its long
journey up the length of the border country and beyond lies the little

town of Montgomery.

To the east the great rolling ridge of the Long Mynd fills the view with its highest point on Pole Bank, and as progress is made along the ridge The Wrekin will be seen to the north east. The valleys provide pasture for sheep and cattle, the upper slopes are wild moorland, or dark forest. Grouse make a swift low clattering flight if disturbed, kestrels hover ever on the look out for their prey and buzzards soar and glide with an ease that is the envy of earthbound man.

A wild country to be enjoyed and respected, here the air is rarely still and in the winter, (and many another time) the wind blasts across the tops with a cutting edge that is Sheffield sharp and the walker that has not had regard to the provision of an extra pullover may soon regret his carelessness.

From Cranberry Rocks, head northwards along the ridge towards Manstone Rock, at 1758 feet the ridge's highest point.

It is an exhilarating walk at any time of the year, although this is no place to set a cracking pace, for the sharp pointed rocks are a bar to speed, and in winter frequent icy spots make it doubly unwise. Like me, and many others before, you will look for the shape that might suggest how the rock got its name, from a distance it looks obvious, but the man proves to be the triangulation point and we must look again, and perhaps like me will come to no strong conclusion. There is a sphinx like outline of a head that is my best candidate so far but I am not convinced. It must join a long list of similar rocks that are eagles, lions, a man playing an organ or whatever which imagination and the right light have perpetuated.

On then to the Devil's Chair, a great curve of rock that is rather more believable in its shape than Manstone.

Another invitation to a better view from the extra feet gained from the top, only a minor challenge to scramble up from the western side but rather more tricky on the eastern face. It has of course the usual crop of folklore legend and fantasy, put to good use in Mary Webb's "Gone to Earth", a pleasing Victorian drama turned into a film in which the young Jennifer Jones starred many years ago.

Legend says that those troubled by having to make a difficult decision, find a solution here. It was necessary to come up here at midnight and dance three times round the Chair and if the sound of

The Devil's Chair - The Stiperstones

the Devil's music was heard, the answer to a question was yes. Always there is the music of the wind to be heard, sometimes soft, sometimes loud - no wonder there were those who could be persuaded that they had indeed heard the music. Dancing over this treacherous terrain at midnight is a sufficiently hazardous occupation by itself without inviting the intervention of the Devil to take a hand in one's private affairs! Certainly there is a price to pay for such foolishness and in Mary Webb's novel, Hazel the heroine falls to her death down one of the abandoned mine shafts whilst trying to protect her pet fox from the hunt. Gone to earth with a fearful vengeance.

This is a sparsely populated area with just a few farms to be seen scattered across the wide landscape, and out of sight from the top there is a handful of houses tucked under the shelter of the hills. Now much more thinly peopled than in the past, this area once supported a thriving mining community centred in the area known as The Bog. All that remains now is the Field Studies Centre, which in previous existences has served as chapel and local school. The search for nature's buried treasure, mainly lead and barytes, has left its mark and the walker will encounter spoil heaps, abandoned shafts and long disused engine houses along the way.

The Devil's Chair gets its name from a mix of local legends, one that Old Nick was carrying a great bundle of stones in his apron for some nefarious purpose and that having rested on the ridge his apron gave way and scattered the stones. Another story has it that the Devil was determined to destroy the bible-reading people of this country and believed that if the Stiperstones disappeared back into the bowels of the earth England and all its God fearing citizens would be destroyed. The great weight of stones along the ridge is evidenced as proof of his attempt to bring about our destruction.

As if all this talk of the Devil is not enough, witches come on to the scene, for it is on the highest point of the Stiperstones - that is Manstone Rock not the Chair - that they were reputed to gather each year to elect a leader. Then there is the story dating back to the eleventh century concerning Edric, very much a local hero who, lost on one stormy night on the Stiperstones, chanced upon a house filled with beautiful young women. Bewitched by their music he falls in love with one of their number and takes her away to be his wife. She is no ordinary young girl and warns him never to question her absences from home, when presumably she is off visiting her sisters at the Stiperstones. As in all good legends the day comes when, exasperated by her absence, he demands an explanation. The lady, of course, vanishes for ever, leaving Edric to a melancholy death. There are other legends connected with "Wild Edric", the huntsman who still haunts these hills, and all in all it is clear that we must have a care when we pass this way!

Onward along the ridge towards the pyramid shape of Shepherd's Rock, just short of which a large cairn marks a crossing point of paths, an especially helpful indicator to the winter walker when snow may disguise the way. Here we turn left to make a drop into the valley, ahead is the blue grey smudge of the Welsh hills. Soon the path loses height, a respite is found from the wind and the surrounding hills close in upon the walker. There are traces of the former mining activities in ruined buildings, shafts, old paths and rail inclines with here and there a spoil heap. None of this is intrusive, nature is a master at reclaiming its own, and the work is well advanced.

The scenery is magnificent with the steeply sloped hills coloured in pastel shades of green, brown and yellow to your right. To the left, often without the benefit of the sun's kindly illumination to bring it to life, the hills stand blackly, with just a suggestion of menace about them adding to the atmosphere of the walk.

The path bears off to the right, soon to meet a descending path to the left. Continue your downhill progress passing spoil heaps. It is one of those descents where you are glad to be going down rather than toiling up, for looking back the ridge above looks like hard work to gain.

The signs of current habitation appear and the track is soon running between houses. A curve in the path brings into view the sharp, almost vertical drop and outline of Oak Hill and Blakemoor Flat.

The little methodist church of Perkin's Beach is passed and soon the road is reached with the Stiperstones Inn just a few yards to the left for those who feel in need of its hospitality.

There is a path that runs under Oak Hill, parallel with the road, but it is narrow and not user friendly to those in shorts and sleeveless shirts. To avoid this little local difficulty, turn right and follow the road for about three quarters of a mile to reach a sign which announces the edge of Snailbeach. Here on the left is a former mine building, still with its tall chimney, which has been converted into a private residence.

I had been watching the process of the transformation on various walking trips and had the pleasure of a chat with its resourceful owner, David McKenzie. There were many problems to overcome, not the least the 500 feet deep mine shaft in what is now his garden, now safely filled in and capped with concrete. It seems that the shaft failed to come up to expectations and was abandoned without producing any great return. The old boiler, dated 1860, has been sandblasted, painted black, the great round doors through which the fuel was shovelled making a unique pair of cupboards and no doubt a talking point at dinner parties.

The road bends sharply here and at the foot of a short hill take the narrow lane on the right, at first with a few houses on either side and then quickly rising up the narrow wooded valley. The path keeps company with a little stream, with steep hills on either side, and a similar barrier ahead blocking the way and suggesting the need for a considerable expenditure of energy.

The buildings are soon left behind, a gateway is negotiated and after passing a green caravan of uncertain age, a further gate. Continue forward on the broad, still rising track and about three hundred yards from the last gate ford the stream, soon to pass a remote stone cottage on the left. Onwards and upwards, passing Nature Reserve Sign number twelve. A narrow path leads up to the summit on which Castle Ring, the old hill fort stands. Resist the temptation for the moment and continue forward towards the summit of Blakemoor Flat. When this is neared an easier approach can be made for those wishing to inspect the fort. As height is gained a streamlet is crossed and the path narrows a little and there is a short soggy section. A crossing path by a pair of firebeaters, just short of the summit, takes you right towards the fort area. In truth there is not a lot to see although no doubt a trained archaeologist would think differently.

Having taken a look at the Ring, resume your course for Blakemoor Flat. From the top a dramatic outline may be seen ahead, the misty and mysterious Devil's Chair, its appearance fully in keeping with all the old tales. As the path reaches the saddle, a narrow crossing path is met coming off Blakemoor Flat, turn left with this and head up towards the ridge not far from the edge of a steep drop to the scooped out valley to your right.

When a crossing path running north-south is reached, about a hundred feet under the top of the ridge, turn right and follow it as it terraces the hillside. It is a narrow but clearly defined path through the heather giving superb views. On reaching the bare open ground of the spoil tips, at the eastern end of the 1443 feet high Green Hill, go forward a few yards and continue with the terraced path, again running below the top of the ridge. As progress is made Green Hill falls back and there is a view down the route of our earlier descent to Stiperstones village. Again the Devil's Chair makes an impressive appearance upon the eye, at this distance and angle, more so than at closer quarters.

The path curves easterly above the valley head, still a little under the ridge, passing between gorse bushes and gaining a little height. Soon the top of Shepherd's Rock comes into view. A short wet patch is crossed, heading towards the rocky outcrop to the south, and then the broad track from Shepherd's Rock is joined. Turn left with this to meet the cairn encountered on your outward journey.

A choice of return routes is available. Option one is to take your outward journey back along the ridge with its mysterious silhouettes of the rock outcrops.

Option two is to take the south easterly track from the cairn which heads

towards The Hollies, a steadily falling path giving excellent views of the
Long Mynd. When the National Nature Reserve sign number 20 is
reached, pass through gate and maintain your direction. After passing
through a gate with the buzzard way mark sign, continue half right
downhill to meet a broader track. Here turn right and after a few yards bear
right, as waymarked, to cross a stream. After a short distance a muddy track
becomes apparent. Follow this through Gatten Plantation. At the end of the
plantation continue forward to return to the car park in a little over quarter
of a mile.

PLACES TO VISIT

Please refer to end of next walk.

10: The Long Mynd
Carding Mill Valley Circuit

BASIC ROUTE:	Carding Mill Valley, Motts Road, Wildmoor Pool, north flank of Haddon Hill, Bodbury Ring.
MAPS:	1/25000 SO49/59.
	1/50000 Landranger 137
DISTANCE:	5^1/2 miles approx.
TOURIST INFORMATION:	Shropshire Hills Info Centre Church St. Church Stretton and at NT Shop Carding Mill Valley.
CAR PARKING:	Carding Mill Valley. Free to NT members, otherwise £1.
TOILETS:	Carding Mill Valley and Church Stretton.

The Long Mynd is the crown jewel of the Shropshire Hills and
thankfully a large area of it is in the care of the National Trust who
have the interests of walkers and riders at heart.

Careful and clear waymarking at many points are of great

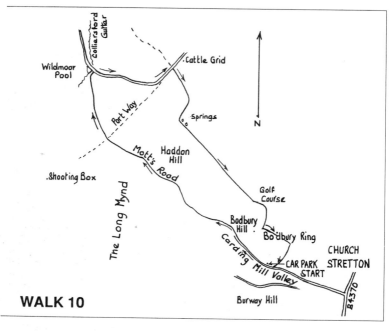

WALK 10

assistance to the walker, however good his map reading abilities may be. In this connection it should be noted that many of the large number of paths that criss-cross these hills and valleys do not appear upon the map and navigators need to bear this in mind. Some of the paths are no more than sheep tracks and may peter out but many others are well used and make a great contribution to planning round walks as knowledge of the area is gained.

The key to exploring the area and adding to the walking repertoire are the valleys (batches or hollows as they are called locally) that thrust deep into the Mynd following the course of little streams and leading the walker up to the high moorland plateau. Despite the suggestion of a long mountain inherent in its name, the Long Mynd is moorland, and in fact, as the National Trust points out in its excellent descriptive leaflet, the most southern grouse moor in the country.

Carding Mill Valley, The Long Mynd, Church Stretton

The Mynd and its batches make excellent year round walking but despite the civilising appearance of the lower Carding Mill Valley, the walker is setting out into upland terrain which weather conditions can render unfriendly, and on occasion positively hostile. The usual precautions for upland walking should be observed, particularly in uncertain weather conditions where snow, low cloud, or failing light may make navigational skills rather more important than a gentle stroll on a summers day may demand.

This and the next two walks will serve as an introduction to the delights of the Long Mynd, whilst in no way pretending to be an exhaustive survey of the area. The walker who follows these routes and notes the destinations of the various paths that cross his way will soon be planning further and longer excursions, including trips over the Mynd to the western side visiting Darnford, Ratlinghope or Medlicott for example.

Carding Mill Valley receives many visitors and it is the first introduction to walking in the area that most will receive. On a summer weekend the extensive car parks are likely to be filled to near capacity, but despite the large number of people who arrive in the valley only a fraction venture much out of sight of the vehicle that brought them. So, if like me, you prefer to walk in comparative solitude, don't despair, most of the others will be left behind within a few minutes, and the vast acres of the Long Mynd will quickly absorb the rest and leave you pretty much to your own devices.

The constant flow of water off the hills has ensured that a mill has been kept busy in the valley for perhaps a thousand years, although initially it was not for the processing of wool but for corn grinding. The carding mill (which combed the wool ready for spinning) served the needs of local spinners from early in the nineteenth century. Later the enterprise was extended to include weaving and spinning, but it was never the large industry that we associate with the woollen towns and the buildings had several changes of use. The National Trust's shop window displays one of the last blankets made at the Carding Mill at the beginning of this century.

Whilst you may be anxious to be on your way and reserving a visit to the Trust's premises for one of their famous cups of tea after your walk it is worthwhile taking note of the news sheet which is issued freshly each month detailing the wild life likely to be seen.

From the car park take the path that runs up the valley that thrusts its way deep into the Long Mynd, with interesting off-shoots up minor batches that hold the promise of further expeditions away from the main tracks. At the final car park the road gives out and a stream is crossed by a little plank bridge. Make your way forward with the stream on your right and the hills folded in great dips through which little streams run down and a score of tiny paths encourage the walker to roam freely. With the car parks and buildings left behind the walker is in a world of steep hillsides terraced by winding paths and narrow sheep walks. Despite the sharpness of the slopes that swoop down into the valley the westward paths gain height steadily making for comfortable walking along clear ways. Grassy slopes are mixed with patches of bracken and stunted trees manage to maintain a precarious foothold before the upper slopes and summit are given over to a wide expanse of heather.

Ignore all temptations to take paths left or right, despite their obvious attractions and continue up the main valley. The path narrows, with an

Motts Road - looking back to Carding Mill Valley,
The Long Mynd

occasional rock step to negotiate as the walker follows Mott's Road, named after a local doctor whose practice must have taken him over these hills on many a bright day or dark night.

A look back down the track reveals Church Stretton between the great V cutouts of the hills but that apart, most signs of today's civilisation are left behind and the young adventurer may begin to imagine he has wandered into a remoter world than the map would suggest. Indeed, a film producer on a modest budget might conveniently locate this as the Kyber Pass, or a highland glen for some epic of the Jacobite rebellion.

As the top of the valley gives way to the rolling plateau the path divides. Take the left fork. Before moving on pause to take another look back to the eliptical curves of the hill tops before they plunge steeply into the valley with Church Stretton seen hazily to the east, beyond which another range of hills close in. As the way flattens out onto the moorland the tent like shape of the Shooting Box is seen away to the left, always a good landmark for navigators.

Soon a direction post is met where three paths run close together. They signal Pole Bank to the left, High Park to the right, but our way lies ahead to Wildmoor Pool. Cross the tracks and head a little west of north over the moor on a wide track which soon changes character, narrowing to the width of a single tread but still clear, even if the heather brushes against bare legs. The long spiny ridge of the Stiperstones makes the western horizon, and in a dip in the moorland, Wildmoor Pool can be seen at a bend in the road.

The path takes the walker to the road a little to the right of the pool, with a small slightly soggy area to be crossed before the hard metal is under foot.

This is a lonely place sitting in the bottom of a shallow bowl in the hills, cut off from the world except for a single track road. The moors stretch for miles, almost to reach out to join the high banked clouds that fill the sky.

The hollow is a natural collecting ground for the waters of the moor and the pool having gathered together the blessing from above, sends it on its way in the direction of Darnford by a stream with the unattractive name of Colliersford Gutter.

From the pool follow the road eastwards, (ie. turn right at the junction of the path with the road) and follow this past the signpost to Darnford until some informal car parking is reached a little short of a cattle grid. A plantation to the left will help identify the spot. From the car parking space take the broad grassy track on the right that runs south east. After a short distance the path divides; take the right fork, still on grassy track. After a further short distance a diagonal crossing path is reached, continue

The high plateau of The Long Mynd looking towards Wildmoor Pool

forward on narrower but still grassy track between bracken.

When a junction is made with a broad track, bare of grass, turn right with this in the direction of Haddon Hill. Continue with this track as it rises gently, keeping a sharp look out for the small stone cairn on your left which marks the next turn left before Haddon Hill is passed. You will quickly identify the path for within a short distance it passes two small springs on your left.

The narrow path follows the upper flanks of Haddon Hill, providing excellent views of the hills to the east. The way takes a gentle right curve as it descends a little at the eastern end of Haddon Hill, but maintain your general direction. As the golf course comes into view drop downhill towards this making your target point the corner of the fence by the large white post indicating the 10th hole.

From the angle of the fence go forward with fence on your left and when the next angle is reached take the narrow but distinct path that curves uphill to Bodbury Ring Fort. As you pause here twixt Haddon Hill and Bodbury Ring there is a fine if restricted view of the Carding Mill Valley, increasing the impression gained from below that this is a little Switzerland.

The path to Bodbury Ring is a narrow sheep walk terracing the hillside and giving quite magnificent views with the streams trickling down the hills sparkling in sunlight. Burway Road is identified as it makes its tortuous way over the Mynd by the tiny cars grinding their way slowly along its steep edge.

When the ring is reached turn left, eastwards, across the fort area, but before continuing on your way take a circuit of this high hill fort, a very defensible area, and offering superb views, especially of the hills that run along the eastern side of the A49, The Lawley, Caer Carodoc, Helmeth and beyond the curving heights of Hope Bowlder Hill running on into Wilstone Hill.

The path from the Ring falls steeply towards, but not to pass through, a wicket gate in the golf course fencing. When this is reached swing right down the deep cleft to return to the Carding Mill Valley and your starting point.

PLACES TO VISIT

CARDING MILL VALLEY SHOP Open 25 March to end Sept and weekends
CAFE AND INFORMATION   Oct. Mon to Sat 12.30-5.30pm.

>Sundays and Bank Holidays 10.30am-6.00pm.

>Closed some Fridays March to end June.

STOKE CASTLE, CRAVEN ARMS: Fortified Manor House.

>Open from first Wed. in March (closed Tuesdays) 10.00am-5.00pm.
>April to Sept 10.00am-6.00pm (closed Tuesdays).
>October 10.00am-5.00pm. (closed Tuesdays) and

>weekends in November until dusk.

ACTON SCOTT WORKING FARM MUSEUM: Daily, April to October.

For fuller list see the visitor's guide to Church Stretton published by Shropshire Libraries and available from the Shropshire Hills Information Centre in Church Street.

11: The Long Mynd
Ashes Hollow and Pole Bank

BASIC ROUTE:	Little Stretton, Ashes Hollow, Boiling Well, Pole Bank, Round Hill (edge) Cross Dyke, edge of Callow, Little Stretton.
MAPS:	1/25,000 SO49/59.
	1/50,000 Landranger 137.
DISTANCE:	6 miles approx.
TOURIST INFORMATION:	Shropshire Hills Info Centre, Church St, Church Stretton and at NT Shop, Carding Mill Valley.
CAR PARKING:	Informal parking - see text for detail.
TOILETS:	None close at hand. Nearest Church Stretton.

There is no formal car parking at Little Stretton but some roadside parking is possible and regularly used by walkers. If travelling from Church Stretton take first turn on right past the Ragleth Inn and at end of lane right again, where it is the custom for cars to be left along a streamside.

Little Stretton is an attractive small village with several interesting features, in particular the little "black and white" thatched church of All Saints. This is not a church that has stood on this spot since Saxon times, but one that originated in the early part of this century.

The memorial tablet inside the church explains ..."This church was built in 1903 for Alice Elizabeth Gibbon of the Manor House. " ......"for more than thirty years she devoted her life to the people of Little Stretton. Beloved in the village she carried comfort and happiness wherever she went. Her life was an inspiration to all who knew her. Died Feb 19 1932". There can be relatively few people to whom such words can be honestly applied. The roof was once of corrugated iron, but the replacement by thatch is a great improvement.

The interior of the church is panelled throughout in wood and

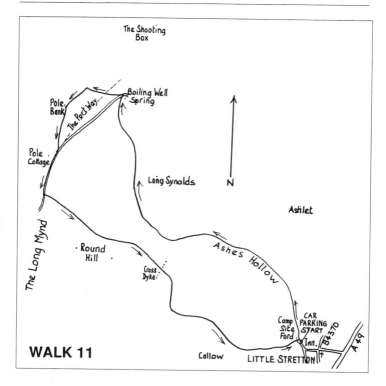

even the font is wood faced. Clearly the church is still carefully looked after and on a recent visit we noted the beautifully embroidered altar cloth, with a crown and roses against a cream background.

Opposite the church is the Ancient House, dating from 1516 and close by the church is the long, handsome half-timbered Manor House. Set beneath the timeless hills of the Long Mynd, the village itself gets scant mention in the guide books and its bypassing by the main road has served to preserve its air of peace. The lack of a car park does not encourage casual visitors to linger and those who come by intent are here because of the quite superb walking.

The route described in this chapter is my own firm favourite of all the Shropshire Hills, although the Stiperstones runs it a close second.

Take the lane that runs behind the Ragleth Inn and after passing Brook House turn left over the footbridge to cross stile on right signed to Ashes Hollow. The path passes through a camping and caravan site with the stream to your right. It should be noted that this stream is followed throughout the first section of the walk to meet the road at Boiling Well. There are, however, several tributaries and it is not impossible to branch off on the wrong route, thus ensuring some confusion. Checking the incoming valleys and their streams should avoid this little problem.

At the top of the camp site, cross a stile by a sign which says "Private property, footpath only", and continue forward, still with the stream to your right.

At the end of the long valley field, cross the National Trust estate boundary.

In a few yards the path meets a rock wall and is diverted over a little plank bridge by Ashes. From here head up the valley on a wide clear path. Ashes Hollow is quite different in character from the Carding Mill Valley, with a personality of its own which somehow seems softer and kinder, although the enclosing hills are just as steep. To the right are the slopes of Ashlet, then Yearlet and to the left, Nills and Grindle. The path keeps close company with the stream, in truth there is nowhere else for it to go, sometimes crossing and recrossing from bank to bank.

As progress is made other batches run into the main valley, each with narrow paths running alongside the streams, offering opportunities for further exploration on little paths, many not shown on the map. This is an invitation that can be accepted as experience of the topography is gained. Later on in this walk we shall look down upon part of our outward route, giving a better impression of how it fits into the jigsaw of the landscape than is gained from the restricted views of these lower levels.

Further up the valley the stream has to be paddled across; a good opportunity to test the waterproof quality of your boots. At one point the valley narrows dramatically, so that the walker is hemmed into what for want of a better word is best described as a gutter. The hills rise steeply from the notch with room only for the stream and little enough room for the path. I wonder if the path totally disappears at this point after an exceptionally heavy storm or a fast thaw following a bad winter?

The Long Mynd is in the care of The National Trust.
Ashes Hollow, Little Stretton

Certainly there is no problem of wayfinding, you are channelled into the only possible route. At the end of the narrow gully, the stream divides and so do the paths. Take the left fork to follow at times a twisting winding track in sympathy with the stream as it comes tumbling fresh and clear down the hillside. After a few steps the opposite bank must be followed for a few yards before returning to the right bank. (This will confirm that you are on the right route.)

Again the steep sides of the hills close in to squeeze the walker, almost vice-like, in the bottom v of the valley with now and again a little scramble to assist progress.

Soon the brief but enjoyable rough and tumble gives way to a narrow but clear and easily walked track with the valley opening out, but still deep in the womb of the hills and with a restricted horizon which is bounded by the encircling hills.

Above the rim of this tiny world the silent birds of the Midland Gliding Club soar high, offering man something of the freedom of the birds of the air.

As the valley opens out, the slopes of the hills are seen to be covered with a mix of grass, bracken and heather with the ubiquitous stumpy hawthorn getting a foothold where it can.

Remain with the clear path that has the stream to your left and as you progress more northerly ignore all diversions along other streams.

The stream and the walker arrive at its source, Boiling Well, close to the road. It is well named, a squelchy area with a scummy top like a great green jam pan. More than one sheep has injudiciously set foot here and has passed the point of no return as sometimes evidenced by the sad sight of a sodden woolly carcass half submerged in the spring. But the walker is in no danger, for a clear path alongside takes him dryshod to the road.

Now we are out on the high rolling moorland plateau, with boundaries of the horizon rolled back, even The Wrekin can be seen, peeping chad like over the top of the moors to the north east. Little tracks through the heather are trail-blazed by untidy strands of wool, combed out of the sheep as they passed by.

At Boiling Well the now familiar square post waymark directs you to Pole Bank. Follow a broad track through the great carpet of heather. The rising and falling contours of the moorland must be a surveyor's nightmare, with the land crinkled, folded and rolling out in many curves wherever you look.

At the top of the rise the long ridge of the Stiperstones comes into view, its lower slopes green pastures whilst the darker colours of the forest plantations and blackness of the heather delineate the higher ground. Corndon Hill pimple pointed at one end, is seen just across the Welsh border.

Pole Bank is achieved by a left turn on a broad track guarded by two posts designed to keep vehicles off the top and soon the walker is on the summit of the Long Mynd, 1692 feet above sea level and promising great views.

A topograph celebrating the diamond jubilee of the founding of the Council for the Protection of Rural England in 1986 directs the eye to distant peaks that are only too often obscured by heat haze, low rain clouds or mist. Despite the assistance of the many pointed topograph is it possible to have set eyes upon the great bulk of Cader Idris? Snowdon, 101km distant, is denied to us, Plynlimmon 70km, perhaps not - and is that grey smudge the Malvern Hills? We must be content with the certainties of nearer hills, The Wrekin, Caer Carodoc, and The Stiperstones.

From the summit continue on the wide path to meet the road, crossing en route the Port Way.

This is an ancient track running over the Long Mynd, said to date as far back as the Bronze Age, which suggests its use for 4000 years. Certainly it is an old trade route. It is not a name exclusive to these hills, many Port Ways crop up on the map, indicative of an old way leading to a market town rather than a harbour.

On reaching the road turn right, passing the large protective square of trees surrounding the former Pole Cottage and watch for the path signed on the left to Little Stretton, which is reached in about 400 yards from the cottage site. From here a generally south-easterly direction is followed for over two miles to make a return to Little Stretton, a high level route that is scenically very rewarding.

Heather moorland has a special character which the Long Mynd shares with parts of the North York Moors National Park, sections of the Pennines or parts of Dartmoor and Exmoor. Here in mid-week there are few people around and you may tread a quiet and lonely track with the breeze whispering through the heather. When a hazy sky defeats the sun's efforts to fully light the landscape the subdued tones become almost colourless until the vast carpet of heather blooms and the moors come into their days of glory.

*Little Stretton and Ragleth Hill -
seen from the northern flanks of Callow*

At first the return route to Little Stretton pursues a broad and rutted track along the plateau passing the twin summits of Round Hill to your right. Take care not to be diverted when the track swings right curving towards Round Hill but keep forward on a narrow track which passes along the flank of the next hill, which soon broadens.

After a while the land on your left falls steeply down to the Ashes Hollow route and your outward path can clearly be seen winding through the valley over 400 feet below. The path swings a little to the right, pulling away from the edge and dips a little before rising to pass through a break in Cross Dyke, to run high above Barrister's Batch and Callow Hollow, each with its blue veined stream. The wide track is easy to follow with no temptations to stray off on misleading paths.

The path dips a little as the huge mound of Callow is approached but passed on your right. Soon Little Stretton is seen ahead and beyond the *sharp pointed southern end of Ragleth Hill.*

The path passes beneath the summit of Callow on the right and above Small Batch on the left. The terraced way opening up to give a long prospect of the hills keeping company with the A49. When a fence is met maintain direction keeping it to your right and dipping down towards the stream below with its short row of willows. Pass through a five barred gate and go forward soon to ford the stream and join a lane by the camp site, close to your starting point.

PLACES TO VISIT

Please see last walk.

12: The Long Mynd
Minton and The Packhorse Way

BASIC ROUTE:	Minton, Packetstone Hill, Minton Hill, with return by Minton Batch.
MAPS:	1/25,000 SO49/59
	1/50,000 Landranger Sheet 137
DISTANCE:	5 miles approx.
TOURIST INFORMATION:	Shropshire Hills Info Centre, Church Street, Church Stretton and at NT Shop, Carding Mill Valley.
CAR PARKING:	See opening text.
TOILETS:	Nearest Church Stretton.

Minton is a tiny village, a hamlet really, lying back from the A49, access is by narrow winding lanes from either Marshbrook about a mile to the south-east or from Little Stretton a similar distance to the north-east. A trawl through the library's assembled ranks of history and guide books produced scarcely an enlightening word about Minton save a brief reference to the Domesday Book that suggested

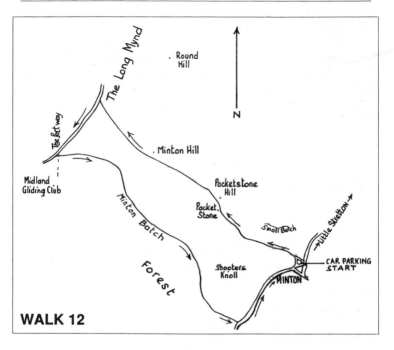

WALK 12

it was well and truly at the bottom of the list of revenue raising locations...."..."waste it is". Today's visitor will have a better appreciation of this peaceful spot with its mix of stone, brick and half timbered houses and a modern-day long house formed by a barn conversion. Birds sing in orchestrated harmony around the tiny village green bright with daffodils in spring and it is with some reluctance that the walker is obliged to park his car here. I can understand the need to keep these villages free of further development but surely it would be helpful to both residents and visitors in Little Stretton and Minton if space could be found for a discreet car park so that walkers can set off into the hills with a clear conscience.

From the green take the lane indicated by a No Through Road sign which obscures a bridleway sign. After a few yards turn left up lane for a short

Minton - village under The Long Mynd

distance to pass through a gateway to enter the National Trust's Minton Hill property.

Make your way uphill by an old quarry with views to your right of Ragleth Hill and further up the A49, Caer Carodoc. The views improve as quickly as breath is lost. As the fences fall back continue ahead, climbing steadily with Small Batch to your right.

When the path reaches the point where paths from Small Batch rise to meet it turn left and take grassy track that rises to Packetstone Hill seen clearly ahead.

This is an old pack horse route and the rock gets its name from the local tradition that this is the spot where the animals were rested and their harnesses adjusted. The pack horse was an important way of transporting goods for hundreds of years, a sort of European version of the camel train. Whilst some of the old routes have been swallowed up by modern roads there are many trails over the hills, now used by walkers, along which the lines of pack animals made their way.

From the Packet Stone there is a wide view to the east with the hills ranging along the A49. To the south-west the forest, looking like the green hairy head of a giant, comes tumbling down the hillside into Minton Batch. More westerly the bare hills carry the planes of the Midland Gliding Club. Below and heading down towards the forest is the deep declivity of Windy Batch.

From the Packet Stone continue in a north-westerly direction with the path fading a little but still gaining height. The path narrows to follow the edge of the rim above the steep slopes running down to Windy Batch. Above the Batch the path divides. Take the right fork which in about a hundred yards will bring you to a small cairn marking the start of a broad track heading north-westerly to meet the road after about a mile. Note the cairn is about 20 yards from the edge of the rim above Windy Batch and care should be taken not to swing too far to the left along the top of the Batch.

The wide track runs across the rolling moorland plateau of Minton Hill still rising a little. The airfield of the Midland Gliding Club comes into closer view.

On reaching the road turn left, signed to Plowden and follow the grassy verge for half a mile to reach the boundary of the Gliding Club.

When the Gliding Club notice is seen ahead take the path signed to Minton Batch on the left. Soon it meets a small stream which will be your companion for the next two miles until the road is reached. It doesn't matter which side of the stream you follow at first but eventually you will be obliged to have it on your right.

Soon you are dipping beneath the hills into a constricted world of grassy slopes, with rushes along the moist edges of the gutter (ugly word that) carrying the water off the slopes. Stunted trees dot the hillsides, rocks outcrop here and there. A nicely remote and enjoyable descending path. The stream is tiny and it is a surprise to find relatively large fish so close to its source.

The forest edge is reached and the boundary followed on your right, dark ranks of trees, standing shoulder to shoulder with just a glimpse of sun over the top or breaking through to light the narrow passage of a firebreak. The stream coming in from Windy Batch adds its contribution to the waters of Minton Batch and after the forest has retreated a single gorse bush marks the entry to Rams Batch with Shooters Knoll standing high above.

When the farm is met at the foot of the hill continue forward, crossing a cattle grid, keeping to the broad track with the stream on your right. A small footbridge is met and crossed to swap the stream to your left. Maintain direction until a junction is made with a lane. Here turn left to reach Minton in about half a mile.

It is a delightful little lane, edged with wild flowers, mouse-ear chickweed, herb robert, violets, buttercups, bluebells, speedwell (surely the walkers emblem, unless that should be the wayfarers tree) yellow archangel, forget-me-not, and a late celandine.

PLACES TO VISIT

Please refer to walk ten.

13: The Three Hills Walk

BASIC ROUTE:	Church Stretton, Helmeth, Cwms Farm, Willstone Hill, Hope Bowdler Hill, Hope Batch, Hope Bowdler, Church Stretton.
MAPS:	1/25,000 SO49/59
	1/50,000 Landranger Sheet 137
DISTANCE:	5½ miles approx.
TOURIST INFORMATION:	Shropshire Hills Info Centre, Church Street, Church Stretton and at NT shop, Carding Mill Valley.
CAR PARKING:	Easthope Road, Church Stretton.
TOILETS:	ditto.

The walks in the previous chapters have provided a number of viewpoints from which the hills lining the east side of the A49 have been a very visible part of the landscape, and like the grass on the other side of the track, an incentive for further exploration. This next walk touches upon three of those hills, and provides an excellent prospect of the Shropshire countryside.

From the car park turn left along Easthope Road, then right into

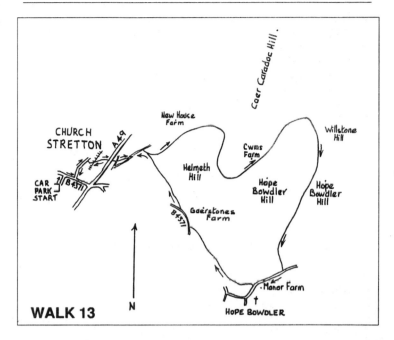

WALK 13

CHURCH STRETTON

CAR PARK START

New House Farm

Caer Caradoc Hill

Helmeth Hill

Cwms Farm

Willstone Hill

Hope Bowdler Hill

Hope Bowdler Hill

Gaerstones Farm

Manor Farm

HOPE BOWDLER

N

Sandford Avenue. Just after the Post Office turn left along Essex Road. After a hundred yards or so, as Caer Carodoc comes into view, turn right, signposted Carodoc and Cardington, to pass behind a residential home. Shortly turn right to cross over the railway tracks; walkers with children should take care to see that they have not run ahead at this point.

Over the railway and a field to meet and cross the busy A49. Again take the path signposted to Carodoc and Cardington, through a small buttercup covered field. Over a stile again to cross a track and up a bank into the next field. Follow the path running towards stile near top right edge of the field to meet a lane. Here turn left to top of lane where there is a beautifully framed view of Caer Carodoc, (cameras at the ready if the light is right).

Go forward to a point just short of the cattle grid that guards the lane to New House Farm and take the signed footpath which runs half right and following a boundary hedge on your right, beyond which is a deep hollow with a dribble of water. Height is gained gently, the path levelling out to

Caer Caradoc with Three Fingers Rock, Church Stretton

pass between the steep tree-dotted slopes of Carodoc on the left and the more amply covered Helmeth Hill on the right. The path continues as a broad track between fences to pass through metal gateway. Follow outside edge of Helmeth Wood, with a pool to your left, where a small group of quietly content mallards have set up home, a very desirable residence.

This is an excellent place for woodland birds, and the sharp beaked nuthatch is likely to be seen, a most attractive bird with a black stripe like an extended eyelash running from beak to back of its head. It is a nut and small insect eater and has perfected the technique of descending trees head first. It gets its name from the way it uses the bark of a tree as a wedge to hold a nut whilst using its sharp beak to get at the kernel.

When the path divides to cross a stream ignore left fork and continue forward for a short distance and just before the track fords the stream, bear right up a slope to pass through a wicket gate. Continue uphill with the boundary fence of Helmeth Wood to your right. The path rises steadily through bracken and tree covered areas. Spring walkers may catch the pungent whiff (politely described) of ramson or the more desirable perfume of the bluebells that edge the wood. As height is gained there are good (not to say dramatic) views back to the steep slopes of Carodoc, its full majesty being revealed as this walk progresses.

When the trees fall back the path swings to the left with a wire fence on your right. Soon it passes through a metal gateway, continuing on to a further gateway at the top corner of the field. Once through the gate turn left to follow a path under the bracken covered flank of Hope Bowdler Hill, with its rocky outcrops thrusting up here and there.

The views are improving all the time, the wooded heights of Helmeth, the massive bulk of Caer Carodoc, the gap between them filled with a glimpse of Church Stretton, the tall white posts of the golf course under Haddon Hill and of course the Long Mynd. The ruins of Cwms Farm are passed on your left. Continue forward on the track which is a viewing gallery from which to enjoy the play of light and shadow on Carodoc's vast stage. Carodoc is magnificent, its configuration closely resembling that of a mountain.

Ignore turnings to left and right maintaining forward direction until a wicket gate is met. DO NOT PASS THROUGH, but turn right, (south easterly) on a grassy track running up the hill between Willstone and Hope Bowdler Hills.

As the path levels out a stile on the left gives access to Willstone Hill, divert here for a few moments to view the world from the rocky vantage point a little beyond the stile.

Hope Bowdler Hill

To the north-east is the steep and shapely outline of The Wrekin, Church Stretton lies beneath the grey green line of the Long Mynd with the Burway Road snaking its way above Carding Mill Valley. The Clee Hills are in command to the east, with their giant matchstick men, which others call radio masts, standing guard above Corve Dale; whilst the long wooded ridge of Wenlock Edge runs arrow like above Ape Dale.

Close by the stile, a scatter of wool in a little wire compound testifies to the summer barbering activities that have left the sheep a few pounds lighter and a good deal whiter than they have been for some time.

From the observation point retrace your steps to climb over a stile and turn left to head south on the grassy track which runs across the bracken covered hillside. The curving path presents no difficulty in wayfinding, since there are no obvious alternatives.

As progress is made across the hill between the higher ground of the summits the view to the south opens up presenting an expansive landscape, very different from that explored in the deep hollows and high moorland of the Mynd. The well-wooded heights of the Edge, the green patterned fields of Ape Dale, not great prairies, still retain many trees in their hedgerows. Trees are something you may take for granted but I know people coming to this part of the country from the fenlands for whom the trees make as big an impression as almost anything else. The Clee Hills become more prominent and the smoke that rises in a great column away to your left comes from the Buildwas Power Station, near Ironbridge.

The path swings a little to the west of south, descending on soft springy turf with the symphony of the hills played by a heavenly chorus of larks accompanied by the more earthly bleating of sheep. As the descent above Hope Batch is commenced, Hope Bowdler village comes into view, tiny and once much smaller.

Head for the metal gateway and take the broad path which reaches the road by a wooden gate. Here turn right into the village, the next turn is to the right opposite the virginia creeper covered Manor Farm but you may like to continue on to the church, St. Andrews.

Local farmers, whilst welcoming walkers generally, have stories to tell of thoughtless not to say stupid behaviour in the disturbance to sheep. Sheep, considered by some to be low on the intellectual ladder, are sensitive creatures, and represent somebody's livelihood. The wool graders at Bromyard can tell a great deal about a sheep from the condition of its wool and the amount of lanolin present. They can spot a sheep that has been prescribed penicillin or one that has had a fright.

Some family connections in this village go back to the fourteenth century. The village is tiny, with a few newish, attractively designed houses representing a small expansion from 1975. Once there was just five houses, a school, blacksmith and, of course, the church.

Hope Bowdler at the time of the great tax survey we call the Domesday Book, was known as Fordritishope and the manor belonged to Edric Sauvage. You may recall that reference was made to him in the Stiperstones Walk - Wild Edric, the Saxon man of title that harried the Normans after the conquest. His lands were laid waste and at the time of the survey, twenty years after the conquest, the manor was still listed as such.

From the church retrace your steps back to the Manor Farm entrance and take the path opposite. The wide track curves left and after a short distance turns off along a waymarked path to left of a barn. The path is followed for just over half a mile to meet the road, where turn right, soon to pass the entrance to Gaer Stone Farm. The stone is prominent on the southern end of Hope Bowdler Hill.

Remain with the road and in two hundred yards take the path on the right which runs north westerly for half a mile to meet the cottage close to the lane to New House Farm, which we encountered on the outward journey. On reaching lane turn left and after a short distance take a path on the right to retrace outward route back to Church Stretton. One last thought, the crossing of the A49 is a great deal more hazardous than that of the railway line!

PLACES TO VISIT

Please see end of walk ten.

14: Caractacus' Last Battle

BASIC ROUTE:	Church Stretton, Cardington Old Road, Cwms Cottage, Hill House, Little Carodoc, Caer Carodoc, Church Stretton.
MAPS:	1/25,000 SO49/59
	1/50,000 Landranger Sheet 137
DISTANCE:	6 miles approx.
TOURIST INFORMATION:	Shropshire Hills Info Centre, Church Street, Church Stretton and at NT Shop, Carding Mill Valley.
CAR PARKING:	Easthope Road, Church Stretton.
TOILETS:	ditto.

Having, as the Victorian novelist would have said, admired Caer Carodoc from afar, this walk will bring about a closer acquaintance.

The strange name of the hill reminds us of the ancient British King made famous in Shakespeare's "Cymbeline". It is worth mentioning that Shropshire has two hill forts of this name, the first is near Clun, but we are concerned with the high and windy ridge that has been in our view at some time during nearly every walk in the hills so far. Spectacular is a word that has been devalued by over-use, but there are few other words that will do.

It is entirely practical to climb this hill from its south-western approach, from the dip between it and Helmeth Hill, but this would be a mistake. It is a great deal more enjoyable to work round the flanks of the hill, ascend from the north-eastern end to make a glorious and long descent over the falling ridge. Caer Carodoc will call the walker back again and again and use of this route will suggest permutations of paths for other expeditions which could include The Wilderness or Carodoc's sister, The Lawley, or an oblique approach via Hope Bowdler Hill.

The start of the walk is the same as the first part of the Hope Bowdler walk described in the last walk, up to the edge of Helmeth Wood but a quick resumé here will save leafing back over previous pages.

From the car park in Easthope Road, turn left, then right into Sandford Avenue. After passing the Post Office turn left to join Essex Road and thereafter take the path signed to the right which passes behind Windsor Place. The railway is crossed, then a field and the A49. Thence over a stile into a short field to cross a lane and enter a further field to exit near top right edge into

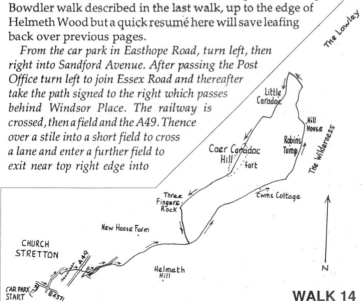

WALK 14

another lane. Here turn left along the lane where in June the smell of honeysuckle sweetens the air.

At top of the lane ignore the first set of footpath signs and go forward for a yard or two to turn right on a footpath just before a cattle grid. (Note: don't set off down the deep hollow way.) The path follows a field boundary on your right, then as it comes to an end the path is funnelled into a wide track between fences and after a few yards passes through a metal gateway with the slopes of Caradoc to your left and Helmeth Wood rising to the right.

Carodoc has its feet in the waters of an attractive little pool; just the place to attract the attention of herons.

After about two hundred yards take the lesser path that forks off left to cross the stream by a small plank bridge.

Once over the stream turn right, for the moment deep in a wooded hollow in the hills. The path soon rises, curving to the left round the lower flanks of Caer Carodoc, soon to meet and turn left on a broader track.

The track is the course of an old road to Cardington, popular with walkers and it also still rings to the sound of horses hooves, giving a taste of travel in another age. The track rises gently, edged with bracken and clumps of rushes where water seeping out of the hillside has kept the ground moist. Carodoc rising grandly to the left and to the right the long line of Hope Bowdler Hill, leading on to Willstone Hill. The views are delightful, improving all the time and the ant like figures to be seen on the top of Carodoc are an encouragement to press on to share the pleasures of their hill top adventures.

About three quarters of a mile from the footbridge a plantation of Scots Pines is met. (Note for future reference, a bridleway is signed off here to the right which can be useful in planning walks over Hope Bowdler or Willstone Hill with which it connects). Just beyond the pines, the ruins of Cwms Cottage are passed on the right. The path dips a little and the slopes of The Lawley come into view.

About a quarter of a mile from the Cottage cross a stile on the left to follow causewayed path running in the direction of the southern end of The Lawley, which from this position resembles, ever so slightly, one of those blancmange shapes that trembled on children's party tables.

It would take a considerable geological upheaval to cause The Lawley to tremble today but we must suppose that just such an

A pause to check the map - with The Lawley in the background

event led to its appearance many millions of years ago. The last violent movements along the Church Stretton fault is thought to have occurred at least 200 million years ago and the volcanic rocks that the walker will have noticed outcropping on Carodoc and elsewhere have been dated to over 800 million years.

A short distance along the causewayed path a metal gateway comes into view, head for this and once through continue forwards with boundary fence to your right.

The long hill to your right is called The Wilderness, although its neatly ordered appearance belies its name. To your left is the shapely Robin's Tump. So shapely that it suggests that nature has been assisted by man, and indeed that may be so since tump is a word used instead of motte i.e. a flat topped mound carrying a Norman fort.

The path falls to meet and cross a small stream, then a stile to meet a track by Hill House. Here turn left on signposted path. There is a confusion of several indistinct paths in this area, but after passing a ruined cottage continue forward for about 150 yards to take a path on the right. This follows the edge of a bracken covered field with the boundary to your left, to meet a waymarked stile. Once over the stile, bear half right with The Lawley looking very handsome ahead. Then follow a boundary on your right. At end of a field pass through a wicket gate and turn left, this time with a hedge to your left. Just short of the next field cross a stile on your left and take the rising path that passes under the summit of Little Carodoc.

As height is gained the views improve rapidly. The steep slopes of Carodoc itself come into view as the bracken falls away and the clear but steep path to the summit is unveiled. The hill flattens out as a stile is approached, giving a view of the northern end of the Long Mynd with the A49 lying below. Beyond the stile a reed edged pool provides water on this dry hillside.

It's a stiffish climb to the top but with the comfort of springy turf and often enough, a cooling breeze to aid progress. A succession of little bumps are met before the summit is reached but the climb, which fell-walkers would account modest, is well rewarded and in a few minutes the walker is passing through the outer bank of the hill fort and taking those last few steps equivalent to breaking the tape at the end of a race.

The walker who surveys the landscape from the summit of Caer Carodoc does so from a six acre hill fort once the home of the Cornovii. It is a high and windy home which is enchanting on a summers day - but what if you were obliged for reasons of security to live up here in the winter? The security is apparent; steeply falling slopes, made more difficult to scale by the engineered banks and ditches, aided by the rocky outcrops used as observation platforms or "artillery" positions from which stones and arrows could be rained down upon an attacker.

Caer Carodoc with its isolated and pivotal position affords one of the best views in the Shropshire Hills, allowing the walker to take in the local geography better than anywhere else. As his eye roams the panorama he can trace the routes of past or projected walks as readily as his finger may run over the map.

In the northern arc The Lawley is the most prominent feature, behind which is seen the wooded slopes of Lodge Hill, from where the eye moves on to the beautifully shaped Wrekin. Below The Lawley lies the little village of Comley. The hills that have edged the A49 for many miles fall back to reveal a richly small field patterning of farmland, broken here and there with small plantations, in winter making the black squares in a somewhat irregular shaped crossword puzzle.

The western view is dominated by the wide expanse of the Long Mynd, its batches and high points seen to perfection and beyond, a glimpse of the higher ridge of the Stiperstones. Beneath the Mynd, road and rail carry their mini cars and little trains, reminiscent of a Christmas display in the toy department of one of the larger stores. The eastern view takes in the full length of Wenlock Edge overtopped by the ever brooding presence of the Clee Hills. Nearer at hand the Siamese twins of Willstone and Hope Bowdler hills, forever joined together, look smaller now that we view them from above. Southwards, the forested Helmeth Hill, is but a stepping stone on to Hazler Hill and then on to the long run of Ragleth Hill. And far beyond all this, and all around in a great and distant bowl, blue grey smudges where sky meets the upthrust land where other walkers on other hills enjoy their day.

Who was the man who gave this hill its name? Caractacus in the Roman tongue, Carodoc in the English, Caradawg in the Welsh, carved for himself a place in history and legend.

In the first half of the first century AD Caractacus was the son of a British ruler, Cunobelinus, who for thirty years or so ruled from his capital at Colchester. Fifteen hundred years later Shakespeare made him the subject of his "Cymbeline". Following his father's death and the Roman invasion Caractacus and his brother Togodumnos, led a spirited and heroic campaign against the conquerors. He and his men were badly beaten in a conflict somewhere in the Thames Valley - Wallingford has been suggested as a likely spot - when the Britons fled, seeking safety in the difficult countryside of Essex. The Romans under Aulus Plautius unwisely decided to follow and were in turn obliged to swallow their pride and retire.

The Roman Emperor, Claudius, arrived with reinforcements, including a detachment of elephants, and retrieved the situation with the capture of Colchester, bringing about the end of effective resistance in the southern part of the country. Elusive as ever, Caractacus retreated to Wales and continued his campaign with a series of raids across the border as the Romans endeavoured to extend and consolidate their boundaries.

By AD47 Ostorios Scapula had succeeded Plautius. By AD50 he was in a position to put the resistance in the west of the country under pressure and in that year the final battle took place. Where? The British Camp in the Malvern Hills has been claimed as the site of Caractacus's defeat, but our hill fort named after this ancient hero seems just as likely. On the outskirts of Church Stretton an area known and shown on the map as Battle Field is locally believed to be the site of the final clash. If so, was Caractacus caught unawares and away from his hill top stronghold, or did the battle range over a wider area with an assault on the fort part of the conflict?

Wheresoever it was that the battle took place, the result was decisive. Caractacus's wife, daughters and other relatives were taken prisoner. Caractacus again escaped and according to legend hid in a cave beneath the western side of Carodoc. Defeated, he travelled north to the land of the Brigantes, but their Queen, perhaps sensing the way the wind was blowing, handed him over to the Romans.

Caractacus and his family were sent to Rome, to be put on show at a Victory Parade. Britain was to the ordinary Roman citizen a mysterious land and crowds gathered for the event. To their surprise paraded before them was not a defeated downcast figure, but a man of dignity with head held high, who had fought a good fight and had lost and in losing had earned the respect of the victors.

Caractacus was a considerable fighter but it is clear he must have been a consummate politician as well in keeping the resistance going over the years of the invasion. It was this skill he used to persuade the Emperor Claudius to spare his life and that of his family. Caractacus died within a few short years but a legend has it that his children were converted to Christianity and in the course of time returned to Britain bringing the faith to their native land.

Many opportunities for photography are presented to the walker with the rocky outcrops making a suitable dramatic foreground to set against the distant hills.

From the fort head south-west along the falling summit ridge towards Three Finger Rock; the reason for its name becoming quickly apparent. Beyond the rock a broad track runs forward towards Helmeth Wood, quickly falling off the hill to meet a broad track at the foot. Here turn right and after a short distance, left over the little plank bridge to turn right and retrace the steps of your outward journey back to Church Stretton.

PLACES TO VISIT

As listed in Walk 10 but with a reminder that if you are holidaying in the area SHREWSBURY although not within the scope of this book, should not be forgotten.

15: An Englishman's Home

BASIC ROUTE:	Stokesay, Stoke Wood, Clapping Wicket, View Wood, View Edge, Gorst Barn, Aldon, Stoke Wood, Stokesay.
MAPS:	1/25,000 SO48/58 SO47/57 1/50,000 Landranger Sheet 137
DISTANCE:	5½ miles approx.
TOURIST INFORMATION:	Castle Street Ludlow (0584 3857)
CAR PARKING:	Lay-by, A49 Stokesay. There is also a car park for visitors to the castle further up the Stokesay Lane.
TOILETS:	Nearest are at Craven Arms, unless visiting Stokesay.

This walk is ideal for those combining it with a visit to Stokesay Castle, providing a flavour of past life in this border area with quite excellent views of the countryside in which it is set.

Stokesay is a fine example of a fortified manor house; a handsome group of buildings of considerable interest and antiquity, deservedly much photographed, and a great pleasure to visit. It might very well have been lost, for such places are expensive to maintain and require much loving and knowledgeable care in their preservation. In the nineteenth century Stokesay was falling into dereliction but happily it was rescued and resuscitated by the Worcester glover, John Allcroft. Today Stokesay is in the care of English Heritage, which at the time of writing, (1989) is nearing the end of a three year programme of repair and conservation.

At the time of the Norman conquest Edric Sylvaticus held Stokesay and it was occupied by Aeldred. Edric declared his allegiance to William but, having thought better of his oath, forfeited the estate.

In the reign of Henry I (1115) the North Tower was built during the occupancy of the de Say family.

One hundred and fifty years later great fortunes were being made in the wool trade, and a Ludlow merchant, Lawrence, bought the

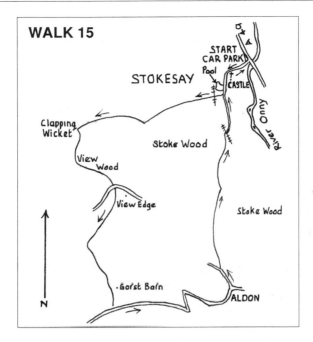

estate which passed on to successive generations of his family. In the Elizabethan era it came into the ownership and occupancy of Sir George and Sir Arthur Mainwaring, during which time the splendid gatehouse was built. The Craven family owned Stokesay from the days of Charles I through to the mid-nineteenth century.

The Midland counties of England bore much of the turmoil of the Civil War, and Stokesay was not excused from duty. In the early days of the conflict it served as a supply base for the King's forces at nearby Ludlow.

Stokesay came under attack by superior forces and discretion being the better part of valour, was surrendered. It was again the centre of military action in April 1645 when it was the turn of a Royalist force under Sir William Croft to assail the castle. A brave but abortive attack that left many dead including Sir William. As a

A cavalry man of the Civil War period photographed at a Sealed Knot Society encampment at Worcester

result of its use as a base in support of the King, the outer curtain wall was reduced in size, the "slighting" mild in comparison with many other places which were left little better than ruins.

From the lay-by off the A49 (on the Stokesay side of the road) walk southwards for a short distance and take the lane on the right signed to Stokesay Castle. A cottage in the lane has a number of imaginative bird boxes on display including a romany caravan and a Swiss House.

The lane passes the church entrance - if visiting the church turn left through the lych gate with its mounting block, a relic of the days when the better-off came to church by horse.

Mounting blocks are often to be found outside inns and churches. I have wondered what people did with their horses whilst at their Sunday devotions....were they tethered to the church gate, or left to graze the churchyard thus alleviating the vicar's age old problem of

The Gatehouse - Stokesay Castle

trying to keep the grass down? The Castle Gatehouse seen framed by the lych gate is a popular photographic shot. The church is well worth a visit.

Keep with the lane as it edges past the castle grounds. Ignore the first footpath off to the right and continue past a pool, and take a signed path on the right. After passing barns on your left go forward and cross a railway

113

line and continue forward on a broad track to reach a metal gate. Enter a field and cross to a stile seen almost opposite, then continue forward to a further stile. Once over this cross a further field to a stile at the edge of a wood. This last stile is hidden from sight until you reach it. A backward glance as progress is made will provide good views of Stokesay and the rolling countryside, but the best is yet to come.

A few paces into the wood turn right along a bracken and conifer edged path which is followed for just under half a mile to reach Clapping Wicket. Emerge from the wood by large ash trees and an old house, now being restored to good health.

On leaving the wood go forward a few paces then turn left uphill towards (but not to enter) the wood. On reaching the fence bear right, following the outside edge of the wood with excellent views to the west. At end of the field cross a stile and continue almost to the end of the next field to join a broad track on the left. Follow it through the wood. Emerge into the open after about two hundred yards. Here bear left up the hillside with the wood on your left. Close to the top of the rise join a narrow way-marked path which enters the wood to meet a clearer path. Turn right, climbing through a hollow way to reach a waymarked stile. Once over the stile continue forward on what in summer is an overgrown path to meet the road by View Edge Farm with its well tended gardens.

The westward views are splendid and these will soon be complemented by the eastward prospect. Turn left along the lane and in a short distance take a path on the right over a stile, soon to see the familiar shapes of Brown Clee and Titterstone Clee Hills. Follow the outside edge of a wood to the end of the field and cross a stile to enter a further field. Gaps in the trees give further excellent views to the west: a succession of wooded heights which include Sunny Hill, the site of Bury Ditches, an Iron Age Fort. Continue forward with the wooded area falling steeply away, to a stile, a little to the left of the bottom corner of a field.

Once over the stile continue on with a hedge on your left. Almost at the end of the field, turn left through an old gateway into a further field which may be under crops. If the path is indistinct, remember that it runs roughly in line with the lone tree on the opposite hill. At the bottom of the field pass through a double gateway and bear diagonally left up the rise to follow a broad track, soon to pass on your left Gorst Barn (the subject of recent conversion work). Pass through a metal gateway and pursue the track for about two hundred yards to meet a lane.

Turn left and follow the quiet country lane, edged with coppiced hazel and honeysuckle in season, to reach Aldon in just under a mile.

At the top of a hill a sometimes dried-up pond signals the edge of Aldon, a small farming settlement with stone barns and houses and excellent views to Titterstone Clee Hill.

The lane curves through the hamlet and on meeting a T-junction turn left and in about two hundred yards take a track on the right. A high level route that gives good views. Over a gate Ludlow can be seen in the distance with its church tower rather easier to find than the castle.

The track enters woodland, at time of writing recent clearing and replanting has encouraged the growth of rose bay willow herb in the disturbed ground, a great pink splash of colour in July.

Continue through the wood with a glimpse of the River Onny snaking through the valley towards Onibury. On leaving the wood pass over a crossing track and a waymarked stile to descend to the bottom left edge of the field. Here cross a stile and go forward on a broad track to meet and cross the railway, turning left on a metalled lane to return past Stokesay Castle to your starting point.

16: Forest Walking - High Vinnals

BASIC ROUTE:	Vinnals car park, High Vinnals, Climbing Jack Common, Mary Knoll Valley.
MAPS:	1/25,000 SO 47/57 (Pathfinder 951) 1/50,000 Landranger 137
DISTANCE:	5 miles approx.
TOURIST INFORMATION:	Castle Street, Ludlow.
CAR PARKING:	Forestry Commission car park about three miles south-west of Ludlow on Wigmore Road.
TOILETS:	Nearest....Ludlow.

Following the first World War the Government established the Forestry Commission in an effort to ensure an improving home supply of timber, reserves of which had been further depleted by the desperate needs of a war economy. Today the Commission cares for millions of acres of forest throughout the country and it is to them that landowners turn to for expert advice.

The Countryside Commission has announced the creation of twelve large amenity forests close to urban areas. The Forestry Commission will be very actively involved in this work; it has the hallmark of a useful and exciting long-term project.

Whilst many will think of the Forestry Commission as supplying the demands for softwood from its coniferous forests they are very actively involved in the production of other, longer maturing trees, as our walk will demonstrate.

The Commission is generous in allowing access to its forests, welcoming in the provision of car parks, picnic sites and waymarked trails and educational facilities that extend beyond the needs of good public relations. A leaflet, "Mortimer Forest, what to see, where to walk" has been produced and is available from Local Tourist Information Offices and the Commission's District Office at Ludlow. (Tel: 0584 4542)

A feature of the forest is the herd of long coated fallow deer of a

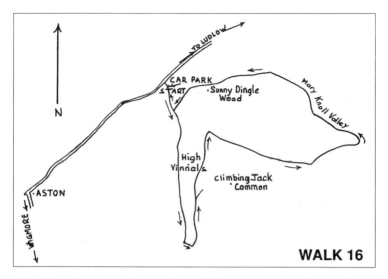

WALK 16

kind found nowhere else in the world. There are some five hundred deer in the forest but seeing them does require a quiet passage along the paths and an element of luck. Watching for their tracks (slots) on softer ground may at least give the satisfaction of confirming their presence.

The walk which follows combines elements of various waymarked routes taking the walker up to a high view point, along broad rides or by narrow paths into the depths of the forest, a pleasing combination which should dispel any misgivings you may have about the monotony of some forest walking.

The walk starts from the Forestry Commission's Vinnals car park to head south. Waymark posts for the first part of the walk are orange ringed. Go forward on broad forest track passing the recent plantings. When a path half left is reached take this for fifty yards only and when it turns sharp left leave it to continue forward as signalled by the orange and white post, passing High Vinnals to your left.

The new plantings which present an open aspect are in deep contrast with the older plantations as the forest path edges the dark recesses where nothing grows under the black canopy.

Forest roads cross the way so keep a sharp eye open for the waymark posts. When the first road is met bear left with this to wind uphill with improving views to the west; a delightful prospect of a score of hills rolling onwards to Wales. Here in the more open areas there is much bird song but as the forest thickens the conifer sections become strangely silent.

About a mile from your starting point, bear left with the orange marker posts to climb over High Vinnals on a broad track. Good views at present, unobscured by the trees which at the time of writing are only a foot or so high. As they increase in stature what was once an airy viewpoint giving a great sense of freedom will gradually undergo the metamorphosis to imprisoning wooden walls.

A pause for breath at the summit offers an expansive all round picture of the Shropshire landscape. To the west more forest plantations and beyond the plain half a hundred hills rolling on into the deep horizon. To the east the Clee Hills hold the stage and to the north the Long Mynd and its acolytes.

Having enjoyed the view and carefully scanned the forest edges for a sight of the deer, continue forward losing height gently at first then more steeply as the path narrows. When a slightly wider crossing path is reached forsake the orange route (this would return you to the car park) and turn right with the green marked posts. The way climbs for a short while before falling over the open Climbing Jack Common. It is worth noting the variety of grasses, some looking their most delicate and appealing as their seed heads mature. Bracken and bilberry edge the path and the tiny yellow tormentil raises its head along the path.

The more open aspect offers a view of the forest at many stages of growth, from infancy to trees in their prime. The path falls towards the forested area and soon the walker is beneath the trees again. On the moister ground continue to watch for deer tracks, this may well be all you will see of them. After crossing forest road the path narrows following a deep hollow way with the bedrock under foot.

Emerging from the hollow way the path meets the "white" route. Turn left with this following the green and white ringed posts. There is a plantation of oak with some birch.

The "green and white" path descends to meet a broad track running through the Mary Knoll Valley. Turn left along this with a little stream to your right. Soon the white track is abandoned as it crosses the stream and you should continue with the green route which follows a broad metalled *track back to your starting point, with the conifers giving way to further oak plantations.*

The waymarked walks in Whitcliffe Wood and High Vinnals offer a choice of six routes varying in distance from 1 mile to 10. Further waymarked forest walking is on offer at Bury Ditches - three walks of $1^{1}/4$ miles to $3^{1}/4$ miles and at Croft Ambrey. These walks visit hill forts.

17: Offa's Dyke

BASIC ROUTE:	Knighton, Teme bank, Panpunton Hill, Cwm-sanaham Hill, Brynorgan, eastern flank Cwm-sanaham and return as outward.
MAPS:	1/25,000 SO 27/37 (Pathfinder 950) 1/50,000 Landranger 137
DISTANCE:	7 miles approx.
TOURIST INFORMATION:	Knighton Heritage Centre, West Street.
CAR PARKING:	Bottom of Crabtree Lane off West Street.
TOILETS:	In park behind Heritage Centre.

If Offa had not built his Dyke, and more importantly if his name had not become irremovably attached to it, then it is doubtful if he would be known to many people.

Offa came to the throne of Mercia in 757AD and during the course of a reign which spanned forty years, achieved recognition beyond the strict bounds of his territory, creating what we would today call a sphere of influence, and becoming generally known as the King of the English.

The length of his reign must surely confirm Offa as an astute ruler with both military and political skills. In those distant days it is scarcely likely that he would have survived so long without both those attributes in generous measure. He came to power at a time of upheaval. His almost immediate predecessor, Aethelbald, had enjoyed a long and largely peaceful reign, from 716AD, but towards

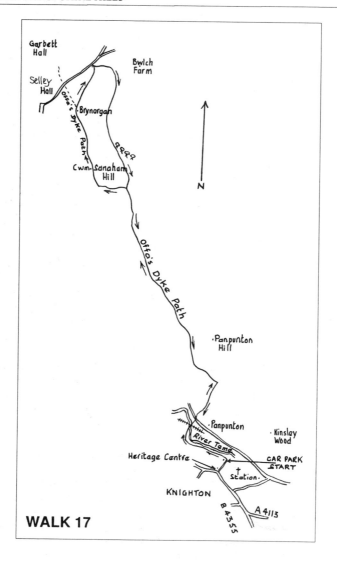

WALK 17

the end of that time his hold upon the country from the Humber southwards was considerably weakened. Three years before Aethelbald's violent death, murdered apparently by those entrusted with his protection, he had sustained a substantial defeat at Burford. As a result, Wessex operated under its own rule, the Welsh were becoming increasingly difficult and the East-Angles, East Saxons and the Kentish men no longer bowed the knee. A shrinking and vulnerable kingdom, which was a prize for the taking or easy pickings for raiders was how it might have appeared to those with coveteous eyes.

"Uneasy lies the head that wears a crown" is Shakespeare's oft quoted line from Henry VI, but it could equally well have been written for Offa coming to the throne in a period of violent unrest that followed Aethelbald's death. Clearly there was a need to put his house in order, strengthen his kingship and make it safe from attack from within and without. He seems to have spent fourteen careful, patient years doing just that.

Not until Offa's home base was strong and secure did he set out to recoup lost territory, pushing out the borders of Mercia once again. 771AD marked the conquest of the Hestingi (of Sussex), four years later the Kentish forces were defeated at Otford and henceforth bent the knee. The East-Saxons gave way to him and London was his. He turned his attentions to the West-Saxons and defeated their king, Cynewulf at Benson on the Thames. This victory opened up the way to the recovery of land lost by Aethelbald following his defeat at the Battle of Burford in 754. Oxford and the land to its north came under Offa's control together with the high downland rising above the Thames from Goring, territory well known, and loved, by walkers heading west along the Ridgeway Path.

The Welsh were next to be obliged to retreat, and Offa secured the land beyond the River Severn, freeing it from the incursions to which it had been subject. He drew a line upon the ground making a clear statement that beyond this they should not pass. This was Offa's Dyke, a political and defensive frontier earthwork that stretched from the Dee in the North to the Wye's junction with the Severn in the South. This determination to impose the rule of law brought peace and harmony to the borders....but not for ever.

If all this sounds like a warrior king, then we must redress the balance with a brief reference to his other accomplishments. Offa's activities brought stability, Pope Hadrian is known to have acknowledged him as the King of the English. He is said to have been a religious man, generous to the monastic institutions. He arranged a yearly payment to assist the poor of Rome and to provide lighting in St Peters. In this connection some writers suggest that in effect he established the precedent for "Peter's Pence" a tax that was levied for over six hundred years until Henry VIII brought about the split with Rome.

A country is often judged by the strength of its currency, (then as today,) Offa was responsible for the minting of the silver penny, which of course bore the king's head to vouch for its authenticity. They came into wide useage, an undoubted mark of confidence in the stability of the established government.

The building of the dyke was a considerable enterprise; that it was carried to a satisfactory conclusion and apparently achieved the desired effect can only reinforce the impression that Offa was of considerable resolve, strength and ability.

That he apparently died peacefully was in itself the greatest tribute to his restoration of order to a troubled kingdom. He is said to have been buried in a chapel near Bedford but there is no shrine to which those minded to do so can make a pilgrimage. In remembering that it was defensive, that it brought peace and stability (for a time at least) to the borderland, we may like to think of his Dyke as a more fitting memorial.

Offa's Dyke was a natural choice for a long distance footpath, National Trail as they are now called. In its 168 mile journey along the border country, it passes through two "areas of outstanding natural beauty" and touches upon the Brecon Beacons National Park. There is a variety of scenic contrast from river valleys to high moorland. It should not be thought that the path follows the dyke throughout, (indeed there is only about 80 miles of the dyke visible) but the spirit of the path is always present. Those who know the deep ditch and bank of the Wansdyke in Wiltshire, for example, may be a little disappointed in the dyke itself. The dyke as seen today is never quite as dramatic as might be expected and can in many places be only described as modest. So much so that on a recent walk in the Knighton area I fell into conversation with two

The Teme Valley from Offa's Dyke. Nr. Knighton

walkers. I asked where they were heading and was told that they were looking for the dyke.....I was obliged to tell them that they had been walking on it for the last mile! Never fear it's not always quite so invisible.

In this book we can only sample a short stretch of Offa's Dyke Path as it passes through the rather arbitary boundaries chosen to illustrate the walking pleasures available in this area of the Midlands. Those who having tasted of the fruit feel moved to pursue it further are referred to the Offa's Dyke Association, West Street Knighton, Powys (Tel: 0547 528753) which has a variety of publications available to assist the traveller in planning his way and selecting accommodation.

The walk starts from the car park at the foot of Crabtree Lane, Knighton, (Off West Street) close to the River Teme.

A visit to the Heritage Centre close by in West Street will be of interest (times at end of chapter). The park has stones commemorating the opening of "Llwybr Clawdd Offa, Offa's Dyke Path, from Prestatyn to Sedbury Cliffs, 168 miles opened here July 10 1971 by Lord Hunt, CBE. DSO" and a further stone erected by the Offa's Dyke Association which is inscribed "Clawdd Offa, Offa's Dyke, King of Mercia 757-796 AD marks the 80 miles of the boundary of Wales, the most impressive work of the old English King."

At the outset it should be suggested that the best of the walk might have its greatest appeal by simply following the acorn waymarked route for as long as you feel inclined and then retracing your steps back to Knighton. Nevertheless, an alternative is offered here; even so it involves retracing a good stretch of your outward route.

From the car park head upstream along the riverside path soon passing a Welcome to Wales sign - which we are in fact just leaving! The path follows the river, via a series of kissing gates, for about a quarter of a mile.

In summer it is a delight to watch the river activity, swifts swoop and dive in an amazing display of high speed aerobatics as they feed off the insects and the no less attractive wagtails are to be seen.

Cross the river by a footbridge then immediately over the railway track to a stile, at first almost hidden by the bridge wall. In fifty yards the path bears right and crosses a further stile seen a short distance ahead. After crossing a lane pass through a metal gateway. From here a long steep climb begins, your payment for the pleasure of the views which are to come. Follow a broad rising track with the wood edge to your right. This steep track lifts the walker high above the Teme valley with views to the shapely hills that fill the landscape, a mix of woodland, bracken and pasture. Here and there presumed souvenir hunters have removed the acorn waymarks, a stupid practice which might be cured if replicas were sold in Information Centres and the like.

At the top of the slope, by a wire fence, turn sharp left as directed by the finger post to pursue a generally north west direction, soon to pass a conifer plantation on your right and following the line of the dyke. After the plantation the path narrows with fence to the right. Knighton is seen in its setting beneath the hills.

The river, looking a little on the dry side in the long hot summer of 1989 takes a meandering leisurely course up the valley, whilst the railway takes a straighter more definite line as it makes its scenic way into Wales.

Level walking for a spell, then cross over a stile beyond which there is a memorial which reads "Roy Waters, Tref-y-Cladd 1970 Society. We remember Roy Waters, chairman of the Society from 1970-1980".

Continue onwards, here the path is hemmed in a little by barbed wire on the fence to your right and natures own barbed wire on the left, gorse bushes, which scratch the legs of the unwary.

When a broad crossing track is met (running east/west) bear right with it for a few yards, then left again to follow the dyke which here in this sloping field looks like a sleeping giant. Another fir plantation is met and a stile crossed to restore the fencing to your right once more.

Continue on the outside of the plantation with the path falling and rising switchback fashion with the triangulation point on Cwm-sanaham Hill signalling the next high point.

As the path recovers some height from its last swoop down, a further broad crossing track is met with 'bridleway' signed left and right. (Note a sign on a gate directs those seeking bed and breakfast or camping to Cwm-sanaham, half a mile downhill.)

From this small cross-roads of the hills take the steep narrow path, stepped here and there, which winds up to the summit of Cwm-sanaham Hill, a good place to stop for refreshment and to take in the view with the triangulation point making a convenient back rest. Spot height 1328 feet, just three miles further on the dyke reaches its maximum height, an extra 80 feet, on Llanfair Hill, where it also improves its image with a more impressive section.

From the triangulation point cross a stile to follow the dyke, pock-marked here and there by holes; ankle turning traps for the unwary. As the fence falls back the path swings half right and downhill to stile seen ahead. Once over the stile the narrow, single tread path drops steeply down the hillside, as directed by marker posts. From here the path is seen clear ahead as it makes its run up to the summit of Llanfair Hill. Closer at hand, down in the dip is the white house of Brynorgan.

Head down towards the house which is reached after crossing a small trickle of a stream. If you have elected to take the partly circular walk rather than a there and back excursion, take the right track by Brynorgan with its rhyming instructions...."Be ye men or be ye woman, Be ye early or be ye late, be ye coming or be ye going, Please don't forget to shut the gate".

Follow the wide track from Brynorgan which runs between hedges of coppiced hazel, elderberry and holly; a nicely shaded lane further decorated *with digitalis and dog rose.*

A metal gate is reached as the path begins to descend just short of the road. Once through the gateway, turn right on a broad rising track. Bwlch Farm is seen in the valley below, the narrow winding lanes disappearing into the distance. Bwlch is just two houses, two caravans, two sheds - and a barn that appears to occupy a bigger area than the rest put together. An old quarry is passed, from which the stone may have been taken to surface this track or build the small scatter of houses. The view to the west has disappeared and the eye is directed to the east, much pasture with the steeper banks of the hillsides forested.

Continue forward with the boundary fence to your left. After a while the broad track disappears but continue towards the long line of trees seen ahead, perhaps planted as a windbreak. There is some difference of opinion between the two maps I have been using as to the exact line of the footpath on reaching these trees. The difficulty is of exit at the top of the line of trees as they sweep off to the east. Crops permitting it is best to keep the boundary fence on your left as shown on the 1/25,000.

I checked this out with the Rights of Way Officer who advised that the Landranger sheet is incorrect but that a diversion proposal is in hand. This amendment shows our path following the western side of the fence until the plantation turns off to the east and from thereon continuing southwards on the eastern side of the fence.

No doubt the proposed realignment of the connecting path to New House (not on our route) will improve matters with, hopefully, waymarking and a stile or gate to clear up this little local difficulty.

As the trees sweep away to the east, leave them to go their own way and continue forward rising over the crest of the hill. Just before a farm building is reached, bear right, passing conifer plantation to rejoin Offa's Dyke path under the southern end of Cwm-sanaham Hill. Here turn left to retrace your steps back to Knighton.

PLACES TO VISIT

OFFA'S DYKE HERITAGE CENTRE &
  INFORMATION OFFICE. West Street, Knighton. Powys.

               Daily Easter to end October 9am-5.30pm

18: More On Offa

BASIC ROUTE:	Selley Hall, Garbett Hall, Llanfair Hill, Bwlch, Llanfair, Waterdine, Graig, Selley Cross. But nevertheless consider dyke only....see text.
MAPS:	1/25,000 SO 27/37
	1/50,000 Sheet 137
DISTANCE:	6¹/₂ miles approx.
TOURIST INFORMATION:	Knighton Heritage Centre West Street.
CAR PARKING:	On verge near where Offa's Dyke crosses road a little to north of Brynorgan.
TOILETS:	Nearest in Knighton.

This round walk follows the dyke to its highest point on Llanfair Hill and after descending to Bwlch makes a return by country lanes and old roads. Whilst by no means without their interest you may agree with me that the walking may be enjoyed in fullest measure by sticking to the Dyke. If walking from Knighton to the triangulation point on Llanfair Hill and back, distance is about ten miles. If the Dyke is joined from the road to the north of Brynorgan, then the trip to the summit and back measures just under three miles.

It is almost certain that you will be passing through Knighton to start this walk and if you have not already visited the Heritage Centre in West Street this may be a good opportunity. There is a display giving the background to the construction of the Dyke and its historical context.

Take note of the various birds that might be seen in the countryside over which the dyke passes, a mix of river and valley dwellers and the high fliers of the hills. The list includes buzzard, grey wagtail, redstart, wood warbler, pied flycatcher, curlew, raven, ring ouzel, red grouse, dipper, and sand piper. A satisfying number of "ticks" if you are lucky enough to collect them all on one day.

The walk starts a little to the north of Brynorgan and is reached from Knighton by taking the road towards the station then turning left to follow

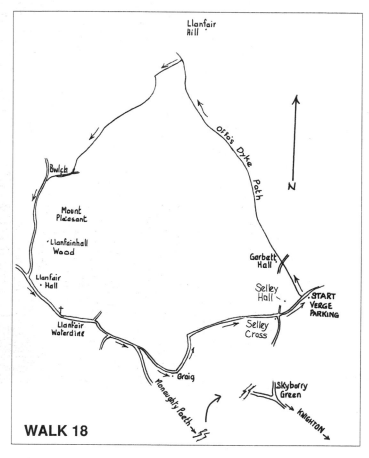

WALK 18

Map labels: Llanfair Hill, Offa's Dyke Path, Bwlch, Mount Pleasant, Llanfainhall Wood, Llanfair Hall, Llanfair Waterdine, Graig, Monaughty Poeth, Garbett Hall, Selley Hall, START VERGE PARKING, Selley Cross, Skyborry Green, KNIGHTON, N

under Panpunton Hill and forking right at Skyborry Green on the Clun Road. There is space to leave two or three cars on the verge of the lane just beyond the spot where Offa's Dyke Path crosses the road near Selley Hall.

The signed path rises from the road to cross a stile, then climbs steeply up hill towards a clump of larch trees, with the dyke to your right. A short steep scramble that soon provides good views. Walk forward along the top

The River Severn near Highley

Offa's Dyke path near Llanfair Hill
Earth Satellite Station on Titterstone Clee Hill

of the dyke and after a short distance lose height, again by the dyke which at this point has widened. Cross a broad intersecting track and go forward to a little plank bridge built by the Royal Engineers in 1985. A further bridge is crossed, shortly to be followed by a stile to meet the road by Garbett Hall. At this point a sign directs you to Bed and Breakfast, tea, coffee and cake, all to be had about a hundred yards up the lane to the right.

Those of you who have just started out and therefore have not earned refreshment at this early stage should cross the road and pass through a metal gate to bear right past farm buildings. The way ahead is now clear, a broad, steadily rising track which follows the course of the dyke. Small gorse bushes add a touch of yellow either side of the track in season and the quality of the Dyke is improving: deeper and higher. Larch trees line the bank and the trek up to the summit affords a splendid prospect of the rolling border country.

The way levels out for a while and crosses a track soon to follow the Dyke to the summit triangulation point which is tucked up against a fence, a little to the western side of the Dyke. The spot height here is 430 metres, but more grandly measured in feet at 1410.

This is a natural turning point for those making a there-and-back exploration of the Dyke. Here the Dyke is at its most impressive and its improved height confirms that it means business. It is not difficult to sit here on a warm summer's day and conjure up pictures from the past: images of gangs of local recruits toiling away with basic tools to build this frontier wall under the supervision of Offa's engineers.

It is very clear from here that the Dyke was designed to look westwards, and however much the line might have been agreed with those who were living on the other side, the control was being exercised from the Mercian side. It should not be thought that the Dyke was garrisoned like the mile castles on Hadrian's Wall; more likely it was patrolled, with troublesome areas receiving extra attention.

(Round walkers read on)
From the triangulation point continue along the Dyke until directed onto the lane to your left, a measure to preserve a badly crumbling section of Dyke. Maintain your forward direction with the lane passing old rusting farm machinery that has long since ploughed its last furrow.

The path and Dyke go marching on to the north but about half a mile from

Offa's Dyke Path - looking towards Llanfair Hill

the triangulation point take a path on the left passing through a metal
gateway. Head about 20 degrees south of west over a field of grass and
thistle, a little under the summit of the hill to your left. A track is met which

curves round to the right, then left to pass through a gateway. Once through the gate bear left with the track rising and then falling to next hill top. It is a wide track with all the character of an old road.

At the top of the rise the track suddenly disappears in the infuriating manner that they so often do, now you see it, now you don't. In its place are two indistinct paths. Take the south western line, level walking on a thickly thistled hill top, so much so that in August when the breeze is wafting away the thistledown it has the appearance of an unseasonal snowstorm.

The hill slopes gently towards a metal gate seen ahead. Once through the gate go forward with a fence on your left to cross a small field to a further gate. Here the track again appears with a fence on the left and remnants of hawthorn hedge on your right. Continue with the gently falling track to pass more discarded machinery; this time a seed driller with husks still remaining in the hopper.

Soon the descent steepens and after bending to the left falls sharply to pass through a gateway at the bottom of the slope to join another track. Bear right, passing Bwlch, a fire damaged and derelict farm, but perhaps still capable of restoration. The track runs down into woodland passing the remains of an old quarry. Thirty paces on take the path on your left which descends through the wood at an angle to join a quiet lane.

At the lane turn left and follow it for a little under three quarters of a mile, shaded by the trees sloping down from Mount Pleasant. On making a junction with a further lane turn left (signed Llanfair Waterdine ¼ mile). There is a great mixture of Welsh and English names both sides of the border, presumably indicating a long period of ebb and flow of people across the Teme, seen in the valley bottom to your right.

Llanfair Hall is passed away to your left.

In a field near here is a large boulder which local legend claims was hurled at the church by the Devil in a fit of pique. I can't claim to have inspected this piece of Old Nick's artillery but supposed proof of the story is provided by the impression of his hands in the rock - he must have had quite a grip!

The little church at Waterdine is worth a few minutes exploration. It features some beautifully embroidered hassocks with a variety of badges, symbols, birds and scenes. Many of the pews have the names of local farms that paid tithes to the church, inscribed in gilt script on the bench ends. The organ is not all that it appears, for hidden within it is an old barrel organ with a small repertoire of hymn tunes; a useful standby when the organist is on holiday! Waterdine is an old border village and its church was rebuilt in the middle of the last century. In this connection attention must be drawn to the finely carved altar rails which came from the old church and carries an inscription in Welsh.

A local legend concerns a young lad who was given the duty of keeping the birds off the new sown fields. This is a common enough country occupation, but on this occasion somewhat thoughtless since it was fair day, and the fair was a quite irresistible magnet. The temptation to neglect his duties must have been nearly overwhelming, but a strong sense of responsibility made him cast around for someone to take over his irksome task. But everybody was at the fair - everybody that is except the devil. A deal was done, the devil would keep the birds off the fields and in exchange would take half the lad's soul as payment to be cashed in at some future date.

The lad ran off to the fair, soon forgetting his bargain with the devil. The fields were unmolested and no one was any the wiser. Eventually the devil called in his I.O.U. before the boy reached manhood, and as a result the young man was buried half in the churchyard and half out. One half of his soul for God, the other for the devil.

Llanfair Waterdine is a tiny village, its population just 12 adults and 4 children, the fate of the village school illustrating the decline of some rural communities. Fifty years ago there were 60 pupils and not long before that a full 100 children were educated there. The school is now the village hall and bears the grand title of Everest Hall, as well it might for Lord Hunt, whose expedition first climbed Everest in 1953, lives but a short distance away.

From the village continue on. Ignore the first turn on left but on meeting a road coming in from right bear left (signed Monaughty Poeth and Skyborry Green, surely we are in a foreign land?) In about three hundred yards take a narrow lane on left which rises through woods and then descends to the farm at Graig.

Beyond the farm buildings bear left on a track signed as unsuitable for motor vehicles and continue with this for about five hundred yards then turn right with it at a sharp bend, a narrow old winding lane between hedges.

There is a long upward stretch between high banks, but what goes up must come down and eventually the crest is reached and the lane falls with the white cottage of Brynorgan seen beneath the hills. The lane meets the road at Selley Cross. Ignore both left and right turns and continue forward, (signed to Clun) soon to meet Offa's Dyke and your starting point.

19: Croft Castle and The Sun In Splendour

BASIC ROUTE:	Croft Castle, Croft Ambrey Fort, Fishpool Valley.
MAPS:	1/50,000 Landranger Sheet 137.
DISTANCE:	3 miles approx.
TOURIST INFORMATION:	Castle Street, Ludlow.
CAR PARKING:	National Trust car park, Croft Castle (to dusk)
TOILETS:	Available for visitors to the house.

For this walk we trespass beyond the Shropshire borders into neighbouring Herefordshire for a "lollipop walk"....a visit to a place of interest combined with a shortish walk which can be comfortably covered in a summer afternoon. The walk starts from the National Trust car park in the grounds of Croft Castle. Admission to grounds and car parking is free but there is charge for the Castle, unless of course you are one of the growing number of Trust members.

Croft Castle is found on the B4362 about two miles to the east of Mortimers Cross (A4410) or about 5 miles to the west of the A49 at Woofferton. Mortimers Cross, although tiny, has an important and lasting place in English history; more of that later.

Croft Castle is approached through an arched gateway in the curtain wall reminiscent of a child's toy fort, an impression that is heightened by the house itself. Here is a splendid mansion, large and square, stone built with great round towers at each corner, its military appearance ameliorated by its Georgian style sash windows and leaded lights. The house is beautifully sited with views to the hills and grounds that are a pleasure to explore. Amongst the attractive features are the Fishpools Valley, an avenue of venerable sweet chestnuts and a walled garden of mellowed brick. Sharing the shelter of these old walls are grape vines, figs, and the everyday vegetables that might be found in any back garden, a pleasing mixture reflecting the continued family occupation of Croft Castle.

To the visitor the house offers panelled rooms, plasterwork ceilings, beautifully polished floors and furniture of distinction from past centuries. Family portraits look down upon you from every wall, former residents of this great house, men who had achieved distinction in various fields, their elegant ladies, and of course the children.

The family's connection with Croft dates back to at least the time of the Domesday Survey. There was a break from 1746 until 1923 when the property was re-purchased.

The church lies so close to the house that on a wet Sunday morning, family worshippers might well leave their front door as the clock started to strike the hour and yet be in their place on time and without need of an umbrella.

The church, with its boxed pews, is full of interest. Its close connection with the great house is quickly apparent. Amongst the memorials the tomb that takes first place is that of Sir Richard Croft and Eleanor his wife. They lived at a time of great conflict when over a long period of years the rival Houses of Lancaster and York pursued their claims to the throne by force of arms.

Sir Richard had battle honours which included Mortimers Cross 1461, Tewkesbury ten years later and Stoke (near Newark) in 1487. It was after this last battle (which resulted in the capture of Lambert Simnel,) that Richard was created knight baronet. Richard was Sherrif of Herefordshire on several occasions and Governor of the nearby Ludlow Castle, but it is the battle of 1461, fought on his very doorstep that takes our attention.

Sir Richard had lent his support to Edward, the recently orphaned, nineteen year old son of Richard, Duke of York. An army of some 5000 men had been assembled and set to guard the road along which the Lancastrian army was obliged to pass and to deny access to the river crossings. It was a strategy that worked with heavy losses to the smaller forces of Lancaster. The legend that has grown up

Croft Castle

suggests that the Yorkist army's confidence had been greatly increased by the appearance in the wintry February sky of three suns. It was probably a manifestation of the halo effect one occasionally sees, that was taken as a favourable portent, and it led to Edward IV taking the 'sun in splendour' as one of his emblems. Hence Shakespeare's famous pun "Now is the winter of our discontent made summer by this sun of York." (Richard III)

A monument erected in 1799 at Kingsland, just south of Mortimers Cross refers to the "....obstinate, bloody and decisive battle ....between the ambitious Houses of York and Lancaster on the 2nd Day of February 1461 between the Forces of Edward Mortimer, Earl of March, (afterwards Edward the fourth) on the side of York and those of Henry the Sixth, on the side of Lancaster.

The King's troops were commanded by Jasper Earl of Pembroke, Edward commanded his own in person and was victorious. The slaughter was great on both sides, four thousand being left dead on the field and many Welsh persons of the first distinction were taken prisoners among whom was Owen Tudor (Great-Grandfather to Henry the Eighth, and a descendant of the illustrious Cadwallader) who was afterwards beheaded at Hereford.

This was the decisive battle which fixed Edward the Fourth on the Throne of England who was proclaimed King in London on the fifth of March following."

The Monument Inn uses a painting of the monument as its sign and at Mortimers Cross the inn signs depict the contestants, armed

The sun in splendour - depicted on the inn sign at Mortimers Cross

and armoured together with their respective badges. Altogether an excellent little piece of history retold succinctly in words and pictures.

From the car park go towards the arched gatehouse of the castle enclosure but do not pass through. Turn right and after a short distance cross a cattle grid by way of a kissing gate, with blue and red arrow waymarks pointing the way. Follow a metalled path and after a short distance bear right with this as it rises gently. Once past a large cottage on the left the track becomes rougher and passes through a metal gateway. Maintain your direction, roughly northwards, passing some venerable sweet chestnut trees, their trunks twisted and gnarled with age.

After passing a further clump of chestnuts enter the Forestry Commission's Croft Wood where a sign directs you forward to Croft Ambrey on a still rising path. When a crossing track is reached, continue forward soon to emerge from the woods. The steep slopes of Yatton Hill to your left fall to the valley whilst more distant hills roll on towards Wales.

Leave the forest by a five barred gate and go forward along a bracken edged track with a fence to your right. After a short distance cross a stile on your right (blue way mark) bearing half left and in a few yards scramble up the steep path onto the ramparts of the hill fort.

This hill top fort with its high banked deeply ditched defences was home to men, women and children of the Iron Age for some six hundred years. Archaeologists have discovered evidence of repeated replacement of the wooden gateways which gave access to the fort; as many as twenty renewals confirming the long residential use of the camp. During the years of its occupation the fort was enlarged so that it ultimately covered an area of nearly forty acres. Within the protection of the compound, which in terms of later years you might regard as a walled town, there were a number of wooden buildings, which like the gates were subject to decay and were repeatedly rebuilt. As we have already seen in the Caer Carodoc walk, this part of the country was coming under pressure as the Romans pushed out their frontiers westwards towards Wales and around AD50 this beautiful hill top camp, which had been home to upwards of five hundred people, became another of history's deserted villages.

This pedestal is erected to perpetuate the Memory of an obstinate, bloody, and decisive battle fought near this Spot in the civil Wars between the ambitious Houses of York and Lancaster, on the 2nd Day of February 1461 between the Forces of *Edward Mortimer*, Earl of March, (afterwards *Edward the Fourth*) on the Side of York and those of *Henry the Sixth*, on the Side of Lancaster.

The King's Troops were commanded by *Jasper* Earl of Pembroke. *Edward* commanded his own in Person and was victorious. The Slaughter was great on both Sides Four Thousand being left dead on the Field and many Welsh Persons of the first distinction were taken Prisoners among whom was *Owen Tudor* (Great-Grandfather to *Henry* the *Eighth*, and a Descendent of the illustrious *Cadwallader*) who was afterwards beheaded at Hereford

This was the decisive Battle which fixed *Edward* the *Fourth* on the Throne of England who was proclaimed *King* in London on the Fifth of March following.

Erected Subscr...

On reaching the top of the bank turn right and follow the ramparts eastwards. It is necessary to duck under an ancient oak which has spread its branches wide and low over the bank. Shortly after this merge with a path coming in from the

The story of the battle of Mortimers Cross, AD 1461, told on the monument

137

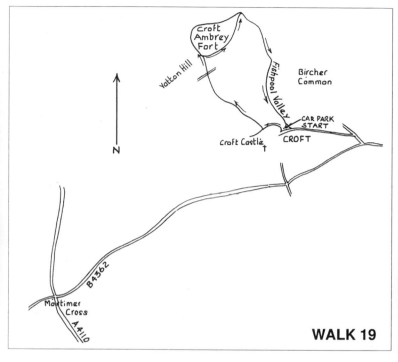

WALK 19

left and turn right on a falling path. A blue waymark confirms you are on the right track. Ignore a right turn. The descent steepens and a small stile is crossed, after which turn right. In fifty yards pass through a gate on the right (blue arrowed) and down a slope to meet a broader track.

Here turn right and after about 100 yards take a forest road to the left which takes a falling, curving passage. There is a good mix of trees; ash, beech, sycamore, larch, Norwegian spruce, and other conifers with honeysuckle spreading itself over bushes. To the right is a deep cleft which surely must carry water but is totally disguised by the thick greenery.

The track curves to the right as it is joined by a broad path coming in from the left. Continue for a further 50 yards before turning right and then, after a few yards left, on a red and blue waymarked path, heading down the Fishpool Valley.

138

Soon the tiny stream widens to produce a series of ponds; an attractive prospect with the trees reflected in the still clear water. Ignore the blue track when it leads off right and keep with the red and green waymarking until after the third pool when the path divides. Take the right branch, red and green marked. The path climbs steadily uphill to emerge close to the car park and your starting point.

It should be mentioned that the National Trust also owns the adjacent Bircher Common and amongst the wildlife mentioned in its handbook are fallow deer, stoats, weasels and polecats which have apparently extended their territory from across the Welsh border.

PLACES TO VISIT

CROFT CASTLE: Easter Sat, Sun & Mon 2-6pm.
April & Oct Sat & Sun 2-6pm.
May to end Sept Wed-Sun plus Bank Holiday Mondays, 2-6pm.
Car park, picnic area, parkland and
hill fort open throughout the year.

BERRINGTON HALL: About 5 miles from Croft, another NT property.
18th cent house to design of Henry Holland and landscaped by
Capability Brown. Opening times as for Croft Castle. Grounds open
from 12.30 (also restaurant).

20: Top Of The Lot

BASIC ROUTE:	Picnic Site Nr Cleobury North, Brown Clee Nature Trail to point 4, Abdon Burf, Abdon Liberty, High Croft, Monkeys Fold, Big Wood, rejoin Nature Trail at 5 to return.
MAPS:	1/25,000 SO48/58 (Pathfinder 931) SO68/78 1/50,000 Landranger 138
DISTANCE:	5½ miles approx.
CAR PARKING:	Road side near start of trail, see text.

Brown Clee Hill at 1772 feet is the highest point in Shropshire and its seniority should by rights reserve a place for it as the last walk in the book. No disrespect to Brown Clee but that privilege, if that is the word, has been accorded to what at first sight is the strangest landscape in all the county.

Our walk includes the Brown Clee Forest Trail, for which there is a leaflet published by the Shropshire Trust for Nature Conservation available from Tourist Information Offices in the area, the Estate Office at Burwarton or from the County Planning Dept Shrewsbury. If you want to take pot luck, then you may find a leaflet in the honesty box at the start of the trail.

To find the start of the walk leave Cleobury North by the Ditton Priors Road, then take a left turn, heading towards the eastern edge of Brown Clee Hill. Just beyond a sharp right bend car parking will be found under trees near the start of the Forest Trail.

From the parking area pass through a five barred gate by the Forest Trail notice and turn right. After crossing a short field go forward on a broad track between bracken and gorse. Height is quickly gained, giving views to the east of well farmed countryside, broken by small plantations.

Continue forward on the track with a variety of trees, if out with the family it might be an interesting competition to see how many can be identified. (Father will supply the prize - and mother the answers!)

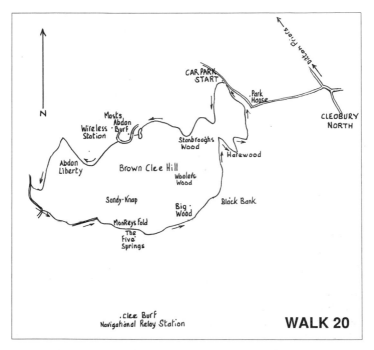

WALK 20

Beyond point 3 a wide track comes in from the right, turn left with this and in a short distance meet point 4. Here leave the forest trail, crossing a stile to head up through woods on a winding track with beech, larch and Norwegian spruce.

After climbing for some while pass through a five barred gate and go forward over a crossing track to take a narrow path through the trees, soon to bear right on a wider track in a less thickly wooded area. The path narrows after crossing a streamlet. Beyond the stream the path curves left and upwards. When a large beech tree is reached make sure you are heading left and uphill.

Confirmation that you are on the right path is given by the humps and bumps of former quarrying activities and with the tops of radio masts seen ahead. A little to the right are the remains of old mine buildings.

A row of stones suggest the boundary of a house and this is

confirmed by a clump of rhubarb looking strangely out of place. How long was it since a mine employee took rhubarb and custard for his Sunday lunch on this high and remote hillside?

As you draw level with the mine buildings the masts come fully into view, their great ears cocked in all directions. There is a confusion of paths/ sheep runs on this hillside but if you have hit the right one you should reach the road by a deep pool. Turn left and on reaching a cattle-grid continue with the road as it curves round towards the masts.

Before the masts are reached climb the steps on the left to the triangulation point to enjoy the view. The hill is on occasions enveloped in cloud as regular travellers along the A49 will testify. In case this provides wayfinding problems you may like to note the road as an escape route to lower levels.

The ground is rough and heather covered, pockmarked by countless generations of mining and quarrying - coal, stone and iron. Fuel to power the sinews of industry. Somehow it is appropriate amongst this guddle of past endeavour that todays communications systems, the modern arteries of commerce, are represented here on this high and windy hill amidst the spoil heaps of the past.

The horizons are defined by the clarity of the day. Guide books have claimed a view over 14 counties. That is as maybe, but walkers who have explored the high points in these pages will at least be able to spot some familiar landmarks. One such not yet visited is Titterstone Clee Hill, lying to the south with its earth satellite station helping recognition. Closer at hand, about a mile and a half to the south, are the masts of another relay station.

From the triangulation point take the path that runs south-west to reach the fence line in about quarter of a mile. Cross an old broken wall boundary and stile which bears the Shropshire Way buzzard. Once over the stile bear right along a raised path which I suspect may have been an old railway. Keep with this as it swings to the right and pass through a metal gateway, again Shropshire Way signed.

Follow the broad, easy-to-walk falling track and pass through a further gateway. After 130 yards pass through a metal gate on the left and head west of south over a field. The path rises but in a few yards flattens out and curves towards a gate in the field boundary. Maintain forward direction to reach a fence and pass over it. (Track and quarry cottage seen below to the right.) Continue forward with bracken on a falling hillside to your right. As the fence at the end of the field is reached the path curves to the right to meet a gateway and the road.

Turn left along the bendy lane and follow it for about a quarter of a mile, passing Brown Clee House. A barrel set at a point where the road bends bears the legend 'Cobblers Dingle'. A few yards beyond this a footpath is indicated off left over a stile. The path bears roughly south-east, climbing steeply. Pass through a line of trees and maintain a diagonal right direction over a field. As height is regained the moorland character of the western side of Brown Clee Hill is seen with its deeply carved clefts through which little streams run. At the top right corner of the field a stile gives onto a lane. Here turn left on a rough metalled lane between high banks. Towards the top of the rise, with Woodbank Cottage on left and High Croft on right, continue forward over a fence to follow what is now a green lane.

At end of this lane cross a metal gate and turn half right to follow a wide path with a fence on your right and beyond the masts on Clee Burf.

The track winds round the flank of the hill. To your left is the strangely named Monkeys' Fold. Continue with the path and when the fence line falls back a metal gate is reached bearing the Shropshire Way sign. Pass through the gate and continue forward to a line of trees and a further gate.

A little to the west the map announces Five Springs. Five Springs, like fingers on a hand, issue from the bracken covered hillside. Cool clear water, rather shallow in a dry summer but nevertheless still running. It is said to be good to drink but recent stories of sheep's liver fluke come to mind and the temptation might be resisted.

Pass through the gateway and go forward on a broad track close to the edge of the wood and heading eastwards. If you are still playing the "spot the tree" game you will encounter oak, sycamore, hawthorn, sweet chestnut and later Scots pine. After crossing a deep cleft the path continues forward, falling gently, then curves to the left as it is joined by another track. Eventually a house is passed at Black Bank. Continue for about half a mile to rejoin the Nature Trail at point 5 as a road is met coming in from the right.

Turn right with this forest road. For the benefit of those without the trail booklet, walking directions are given quoting the stop numbers. The track falls steadily towards a gateway but about hundred yards short of it turn left (by stop 6) into the wood to follow a clear path through conifers for about 300 yards, then turn right at point 7. Drop downhill for a short distance to point 8 and just beyond turn left. In about a hundred yards go half right as directed by a trail sign to meet point 9 where bear half left.

Point 10 is reached by a broken wall, continue forward beyond this to take a path downhill, soon swinging to the left to meet and cross a stile. Follow the path edged by bracken and rose bay willow herb. After crossing a streamlet bear right to a gate and starting point.

21: The Land Man Made

BASIC ROUTE:	Titterstone Clee Hill Quarries - Summit, Giants Chair, Callowgate, semi-circuit of lower flanks to Incline to return to quarry.
MAPS:	1/25,000 SO47/57 (Pathfinder 951) 1/50,000 Landranger 137
DISTANCE:	3¹/₂ miles approx.
TOURIST INFORMATION:	Ludlow.
CAR PARKING:	Close to summit. See text for access.
TOILETS:	Nearest at Clee Hill near view point close to Victoria Inn.

The Clee Hills are rich in mineral wealth and here man, having dug deep into the earth's treasure chest, has in the past scattered the packing and forgotten to replace the lid. The evidence of centuries of the search for coal, iron and stone is seen in a landscape pitted and dotted with an uneven surface of lumps and bumps, the remains of old quarry buildings - large and small. Stone is still extracted from the Clee Hills for road making and a coal seam has recently been uncovered.

This is a walk that starts from the top of the hill (well nearly) so that the splendid view offered from the summit is obtained with little effort for those with their own transport. From Clee Hill Village take the Ludlow Road, A4117 and turn right to Dhustone. Follow the long narrow road uphill, beyond the village and pursue this to the old quarries, turning to the right with the road until a notice forbids further passage except to official vehicles. Park off the road here.

All around is a landscape that has been raided by man and left in

On Caer Caradoc

Ashes Hollow, Long Mynd

The Manstone rocks on the Stiperstones

Descending the old mining combe from Stiperstones to Perkins Beach

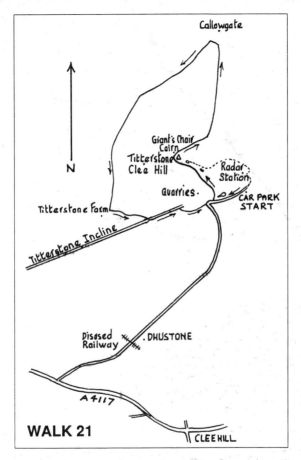

WALK 21

untidy heaps for nature to do its best to heal the wounds. It must be said that the area has a perverse interest of its own. More recent work with the cleaner cut of modern machinery has had different results.

You are parked in a dramatic lunar landscape, an impression greatly heightened by the radar masts and the great white dome of

145

Satellite Station, Titterstone Clee Hill

an earth satellite station perched high above a former quarry. Here countless millions of tons of stone and spoil have been removed. The great scoop of the former quarry is almost neat enough to encourage the thought that we are seeing a partly constructed sports stadium of Olympic proportions.

Turn back along the road for about 300 paces and just past a pool turn right up an incline to reach the top edge of the quarry. Bear left along its rim heading towards the earth satellite station.

Head half left, passing the installations to your right, to make for the triangulation point. From the summit, 1749 feet, the views are wide with a circle of hills fading into the distance.

Beyond Ludlow rise the tree covered hills that make up part of the Mortimer Forest. To the north beyond the mosaic of the farmland rises Brown Clee Hill with its own tall masts. The equipment of the Civil Aviation Authority's tracking station gives off an incessant mosquito like hum and notices warn of high voltage.

Cheek by jowl with today's technology are the remains of an Iron Age hill fort, but somehow it escapes proper notice amongst all the upheaval of the mining operations and the scattered stone that litters the slopes. The area must have been fairly well populated in its day for the fort is amongst the largest with other, albeit smaller, forts on Abdon Burf, Clee Burf and Nordy Bank.

From the triangulation point bear right along the little path to the Giant's Chair, a rocky and uncomfortable seat that looks north to Brown Clee Hill. From here there is a steeply scrambling descent that is best avoided. At first sight there seems no clear path for the next leg of the walk which heads towards the little red roofed cottage seen to the north at Callowgate. However, from the chair head roughly eastwards on a narrow falling path, aiming to gradually swing to the left and navigate a way through the bracken and grass towards the cottage. A reasonably clear but single tread path runs just beside a long line of scattered rock.

Continue in an easterly direction, descending towards an area of bracken and rocks. On reaching the bracken keep an eye on the cottage and bear left towards it and Brown Clee Hill on an indistinct path. There are several fading paths and sheep walks, which like streams falling off a mountain seem to run towards each other.

Looking back shows the ostrich egg-like shape of the satellite station sitting in a giant's egg cup. After descending through the bracken, pass through tufted grass and about 200 yards or so short of the cottage bear left on a broad track (not all that obvious at first - but wheel marks will give the clue). The path heads roughly south-west soon to pass through bracken. The way terraces under the lower flanks of the hill, making a long slow curving semi-circuit.

The summit rises darkly above a sea of green, its upper slopes banded by a wide black vein of rock. The satellite stations appear over one shoulder.

Continue with your track, ignoring all turns to left and right. After a period of fairly level walking height is gradually regained and the path levels out again. Beneath the western edge of the hill ahead, on the skyline, will be seen the steeply shelved slopes of Clee Hill, still being quarried and neatly cut like slices of cake, a sharpness not normally found in nature.

After a while the little settlement of Titterstone comes into view. As you draw level with this the path leads to the old incline that carried the light railway. Go forward to this, turn left to follow the incline back to the hill top. At the top of the incline a crumbling mass of old buildings remain, grist to the mill for future industrial archaeologists. Maybe today's graffiti will cause them more problems than the industrial remains.

Bear right on the mine track with the buildings to your left. The track curves left up the hill and after passing under a broken arch of a bridge bear left with the road to make a return to your starting point.

Appendix 1: Sabrina Fair - Bridgnorth

BRIDGNORTH IS a little gem. True, not all its facets shine as well as they might, but the old market town is full of interesting little lanes and alleys winding their way about the town and its old inns. The sandstone on which it stands is easily worked and there are many caves that have been hollowed out of the rock. In Cartway a plate recalls that caves here were used as private dwellings up to 1856; there are similar caves beneath Castle Walk and elsewhere along the Severn Valley. A number are still in use today and the walker will encounter some garden sheds, a garage and even a house carved out of the living rock.

From the bridge below the town, Castle Mount may be gained either by the Cliff Railway installed in 1891 or by the Stoneway Steps ...nearly two hundred they say. Better still is to walk up the Cartway, following the age old route up to High Town. On the way, Bishop Percy's House is passed, arguably the most striking of the town's residences, a tall black and white half timbered building dating back to 1580. Thomas Percy was born here in 1729, a scholarly man whose career in the church culminated in his appointment as Bishop of Dromore in Ireland. His publications included *Reliques of English Poetry* and *Memoir of Goldsmith* ....he of *She Stoops to Conquer* and *The Deserted Village* fame. Today the building is home to the Bridgnorth Boys Club.

Near the top of the Cartway lies the narrow Castle Walk running between old houses, one with the date 1665 cut into its timbers. As the houses fall back the river scene is laid out before the visitor.

The view of Bridgnorth from the river is dominated by the handsome church of St Mary Magdelene, quite unlike the image of the usual parish church. It is beautifully proportioned; a square tower rises to support a clock with four faces above which a green dome is topped by a cross.

Within the church all is bright and airy, six great windows allow the light to come flooding in, a pleasant change from the gloomy darkness that is so often encountered in churches. Two rows of six columns each support the high roof. It is a place of dignity and peace

River Severn and Low Town from Castle Walk, Bridgnorth

but with perhaps more of the atmosphere of the concert hall than that of a place of worship, an impression heightened by the absence of plaques and memorials on the walls; in the context of this building a totally right decision.

It is a different church but then its architect was a man more famous in another field - that of civil engineering. He was none other than Thomas Telford whose list of achievements include the Menai Bridge, the Shrewsbury to Holyhead road and the Caledonian Canal. Telford originally trained as a stone mason before turning to the roads, bridges and canals for which he is best remembered. Had he continued with his architectural work how many more glorious buildings might he have left us today?

Behind the church is a tower, all that remains of Bridgnorth Castle, tilted at an impossible angle (17 degrees out of true). The town is built on an obviously important strategic position, commanding the roads and river. A burh, an Anglo-Saxon fortified town, was in being here early in the tenth century, with the Norman castle following after the Conquest.

Beyond the castle the view to the west takes in the railway station, and Pan Pudding Hill from which the bombardment of Bridgnorth was launched during the Civil War. The coming of the railway age made a major impact. The river had been an important source of trade and employment, bringing goods and customers to the long established market. The town was one of a number of inland ports along the Severn, the fast flow making for easy downstream progress, the upstream voyage dependent upon the muscle power of men and horses. There were coal and iron industries further downstream and the Bridgnorth wharves were kept busy with many kinds of traffic, until the rapid expansion of the railway network enabled the speedier movement of goods and passengers throughout the country.

The town was itself, in a way, responsible for the loss of the river trade, for just across the river at Low Town was Hazeldine's foundry. Two great names of the early railway age came together here. Richard Trevithick, the inventor of the high pressure steam engine, and the engineer John Rastrick. In 1808 Rastrick constructed from Trevithick's design the world's first passenger locomotive engine, the "Catch me who can". Trevithick had a circular track laid in what is now Euston Square and demonstrated their joint achievement to the admiring citizenry of the capital.

To the north of Castle Mount is the main shopping area of the town, still with a number of attractive half timbered buildings and

Bridgnorth's answer to the leaning tower of Pisa. The remains of the castle with the tower of Telford's church

the town hall dated 1652, its top half looking immeasurably better than its supporting bottom storey. Until about 1750 the assize courts for the area were held here. Strangely, it seems to have been acquired second hand, the half timbered part having served an earlier life as a barn at Much Wenlock.

Off the main street is St Leonard's Church, of which more later. Hereabouts the Franciscan brothers established a Friary in 1245, which along with many greater religious houses, disappeared with the Dissolution of the Monasteries.

The Civil War is writ large in the histories of most Midland towns and villages for it was across this part of the country, as much as any, that the armies marched and fought in little local skirmishes or large scale set piece battles. Bridgnorth was no exception.

In the course of his manoeuvring across country and gathering his army together Charles the First arrived in Bridgnorth in October 1642, apparently to a general welcome by the population.

Whilst the King enjoyed the hospitality of Sir Thomas Whitmore within the castle, his army was accommodated in the town and the villages thereabouts. The King and the army soon moved on but during the course of the campaigning that flowed back and forth across the Midlands the Castle came under artillery fire. Later, in March 1646, the Parliamentarian Army successfully forced its way into the town. The Royalist defenders, following a scorched earth policy, started fires that led to the destruction of a large part of High Town, especially as powder kegs were stored in St Leonard's Church. More than three hundred families were left homeless and without means of support.

We have touched a little upon the history of Bridgnorth. Meanwhile, if perhaps you are puzzled by the title of this chapter...Sabrina Fair...then I should explain that she is the Goddess of the Severn. You will find her on Castle Mount, her charms enriching the small fountain acknowledging the life and work of Henry Whitmore..."Faithful and valued representative of Bridgnorth in Parliament".

Appendix 2: Ironbridge

THE SHROPSHIRE explorer can no more exclude Ironbridge from his itinerary than the visitor to London can miss Westminster Abbey or the Tower. For here, rescued from dereliction and decay, is a complex of museums celebrating in a highly enjoyable manner the birth place of the Industrial Revolution. To further underline its importance, the Ironbridge Gorge became Britain's first World Heritage Site - a designation by Unesco that places it in a small but distinguished company.

Despite its great historical importance it is also a unique family day out, though in truth you would be hard put to fully cover the area within the course of a single day. This has been recognised by the Museum Trust which issues Passport Tickets that provide for admission on subsequent occasions to those museums that have not been visited.

By far the best prospect of Ironbridge is found on the west bank of the Severn close to the Toll House. It is a convenient place to park a car and explore the immediate vicinity of the bridge. (NB: the various museums are spread over a wide area and it will eventually be necessary to move on.) The eye is carried across the river to the town as it rises in terraces above the river gorge. All now in excellent order, with houses in good English brick and a few in colourwashed render, with the church taking a prominent position opposite the bridge, the scene mildly suggesting a continental location rather than Shropshire.

The history of iron is a long one beginning as far as this country is concerned, around 500 to 600BC. The Romans took a hand in its production as did some of the monastic institutions. Production methods developed slowly; water power came into use early in the thirteenth century and the blast furnace was in use by 1500. Iron was produced in many parts of the country, particularly where a plentiful supply of charcoal was available, such as the Forest of Dean and The Weald, where both limestone and ironstone were also found.

Iron had been made at Coalbrookdale from at least 1500 but it was the arrival of the Darby family early in the eighteenth century that

Ironbridge with the world's first iron bridge
that gave the village its name

expanded the industry in the area. Iron had become an increasingly important element in warfare but this was entirely alien to the Darbys who were Quakers and so they concentrated very successfully on the production of domestic items. The invention of the iron smelting process using coke instead of charcoal by Abraham Darby I led to the cost effective production of iron in great quantities and heralded the Industrial Revolution. Seventy years later his grandson, Abraham Darby III was to use iron to bring about another revolution, this time in civil engineering with the construction of the world's first iron bridge.

THE IRON BRIDGE

THE RIVER which served for the transport of goods and passengers along much of its length was something of a hindrance to east-west traffic and the need for a substantial bridge had long been felt. Walkers exploring the Severn Valley today are still handicapped by the less than frequent provision of bridges, so the problems that confronted the architects and constructors of two hundred years ago may be imagined. To bridge the Severn at this point was not easy, the sides of the gorge rose steeply from the river banks and adequate freeway had to be allowed for the passage of the considerable river traffic. A single span bridge seemed the answer if only the means to provide it could be found.

A consortium of local businessmen was formed to further the cause of bridging the river. Architect Thomas Pritchard produced plans, Abraham Darby the third took on the role of treasurer, as well as the responsibility of construction. The necessary Act of Parliament was passed in 1776 "....for the building of a bridge across the River Severn from Benthall in the county of Salop to the opposite shore of Madley wood, in the said county, and for the making of avenues or roads to and from the same". There is no doubt that the project did not get under way without much deliberation and there must have been many misgivings. After all the builders were entering unknown country. Work started in the winter of 1777, but it was New Year's Day 1781 that the world's first iron bridge was opened.

We may imagine that there was considerable cause for celebration at the successful spanning of the river and some statistics may not come amiss. The 24 feet wide bridge stands 40 feet above the river with a span of just over 100 feet. The toll house which stands at the eastern end of the bridge displays the original estimate of the cost of construction which was £3200, which included the provision of

251 tons of iron. In the event a further hundred tons of iron was needed so that the final cost of the project does not emerge. The bridge was private property and a toll was charged for the privilege of crossing the Severn. No one was exempt, a notice made that quite clear ....."......every officer or soldier, whether on duty or not is liable to pay a toll for passing over as well as any baggage wagon, mail coach or the Royal Family". The bridge continued to produce a revenue until 1950 when the tolls were abolished. The charges will also be of interest: The table of tolls displayed includes upon its tariff.."For every coach, landau, hearse, chaise chair or suchlike carriages drawn by six horses, mares, geldings or mules two shillings". The rate for conveyances drawn by a single horse fell to sixpence. A cow could cross for a penny, a calf, pig, sheep or lamb, halfpenny as was a person on foot. There was also a charge for the use of the road (by those not actually making the crossing) at half the scale of the bridge crossing.

The visitor centre lies across the river and to the left and features a history of the River Severn.

THE MUSEUM OF IRON

THE MUSEUM is housed in the former Great Warehouse and is next to the Coalbrookdale Company's foundry, with its tall chimneys still issuing smoke and proudly proclaiming the continuance of a long tradition in this special place.

The museum relates the story of iron from its earliest days, but it is of course with the products of Coalbrookdale and the ironmasters of the Darby and Reynolds family that it is especially concerned. As has already been mentioned the Darbys developed the domestic side of the industry and there is a collection of iron bellied pots ranging in size up to 400 gallons, of the sort that the comic strips illustrated as being used by cannibals to cook interfering missionaries. There are innumerable iron products from the really useful to the merely decorative. Ornamental hall stands, notices in cast iron favoured by the railway companies, a Victorian pillar box of 1870, and a host of fireplaces, pumps, mangles, cooking utensils, water closet cisterns, typewriters, seats, gates - the list is endless.

The construction of the Iron Bridge led to an increasing use of iron in many areas of engineering. The bridge had its supreme test and its value fully appreciated in 1795. In that year the volatile River Severn swollen by heavy storms, lived up to its reputation and every bridge along its length sustained damage.....except one.....it's an ill wind.

Thomas Telford, church architect and civil engineer made great use of iron. He designed the first major iron aqueduct on the Shrewsbury canal. When he was entrusted with the construction of the Ellesmere Canal it was iron that he used to make the thousand foot crossing of the Dee.

And so the story is unfolded from locomotives to lamp posts, sewing machines to suspension bridges, but one other set of firsts must be mentioned whilst leaving the reader to make his own discoveries at the museum. It concerns that other great engineer with the splendid name, Isambard Kingdom Brunel and a ship that was itself full of "firsts". Iron from Coalbrookdale was used to build the first iron ship, the SS Great Britain. Its launching at Bristol in 1844 gave the world not only the first iron ship, but the first propeller driven ship, the first iron buoyancy life boats, and the first ship with a bridge.

Clearly we have touched upon men of great stature and there is one other that is remembered in the museum but not in quite the same context of the word. He was William Ball, for forty years a Coalbrookdale Company employee. His claim to fame was his enormous size. He turned the scales at over forty stone, his other vital statistics including an 80 inch stomach, a 50 inch thigh and collar size 23½. It is recalled that when he went to the Great Exhibition in 1851 he was obliged to travel in the guard's van. He died the following year aged 57 and some twenty bearers were required to convey his mortal remains to his lasting resting place. His chair and walking stick survive to fill yet another interesting corner of the museum.

The Coalbrookdale Old Furnace where Darby pioneered the smelting process using coke in 1709 is preserved within a building a little away from the main museum. Here the noise and tumult is recalled in a small measure by a light and sound presentation, thankfully without the choking fumes and intense heat of the furnace. If Ironbridge was the birthplace of the Industrial Revolution then here is the womb in which it was conceived.

ROSEHILL

ONLY A short distance from the foundry is Rosehill, one of the Darby's family homes. Though they were wealthy people they lived close to the works, on call to deal with any crisis that might arise.

Here an aura of peace and quiet prevails, though whether this is due to the careful restoration of the house which was built in 1730 but now reflects the mid-nineteenth century home, or the happiness engendered by its former residents, no one can say.

Amongst the many items of interest is the partners' desk where Abraham Darby III must have done much of his work on the iron bridge. A commonplace book with entries in a beautiful highly legible copper plate puts most modern writers to shame. Few people can write like that today but even when Darby was still at school the exercise books shown in the museum demonstrate the firmness of hand and clarity of lettering that was a feature of the education of the day. As has been mentioned the Darbys were Quakers and there are a number of books including William Penn's "No Cross, No Crown", written in 1669, in an edition of 1750 and carrying the signature of Samuel Darby.

Abraham Darby III's marriage to Rebecca Smith is well authenticated...the certificate being signed by no less than 65 witnesses!

BLISTS HILL OPEN AIR MUSEUM

IF YOU are faced with the choice of only one of the museums to visit then this is the one that you can be sure all the family will enjoy.

Here on a large site are a number of industrial and engineering wonders of their age intermingled with ..."a small town reconstructed showing how people lived and worked a hundred years ago." This has been a most successful excursion into the concept of the living museum. The staff wear the costume of the late Victorian period as they demonstrate the craftmanship of the day.

To enter fully into the spirit you must first call at the bank and change your money into pre-decimal coinage specially minted for the museum. There is a huge pleasure in buying a cup of tea for a penny or a pint in the pub with its cosy fire.

There is no hassle to read a myriad labels to find out what is going

Blists Open Air Museum - The Chemist's shop

on, education or entertainment is effected by word of mouth. The chemist has his story to tell the crowds that throng his shop, with its enormous collection of bottles full of the mysteries of a past pharmacopoeia, and has a ready answer to any question. The candle maker explains the finer points of his trade and spices it with snippets such as the story of the pig that was kept in the sty next door and fed on the waste tallow.

Butchers, bakers, cobblers, printers, wheelwrights, brass founders, locksmiths and more are there behind their counters or at their workplace to paint the picture in a highly practical and entertaining way of the life and times of everyman in Coalbrookdale and many another small town.

Blast furnaces, beam engines, mine shafts, pitheads with their winding gear and even a little gospel car made from an old tram is there, and more is being added.

There is the comparative affluence of the doctor's house to be contrasted with the squatter's home, built within 24 hours, where a miner and his wife brought up seven children in two rooms. The last of the Trows, The Spry, a river craft unique to the Severn, is under restoration and there are expectations of reconstructing a school of the time.

The museum is a mixture of the commonplace and the wonders of the age. In that last category must come the Hay Incline Plane, a marvel of inventive engineering that enabled barges to be moved up and down the steep sides of the gorge from the Shropshire canal to the River Severn in a matter of minutes.

MORE AND YET STILL MORE

AMONGST THE other museums and points of interest are the Bedlam Furnaces, the Jackfield Tile Museum, The Tar Tunnel and the Coalport China Museum.

Ironbridge achieved renown for its connection with many innovative projects; its museums can be proud of carrying on that tradition. The beauty of Ironbridge is the overriding excellence, not just into the history of its industry but in people who made it happen and those that worked for them at all levels. Here in this Shropshire riverside town is a microcosm of social and industrial history which changed the face of the world.

PLACES TO VISIT

VISITOR CENTRE:	
MUSEUM OF IRON:	Throughout the year
COALPORT CHINA WORKS:	Summer 10am to 6pm
TAR TUNEL:	Winter 10am to 5pm
TOLL HOUSE:	
JACKFIELD TILE MUSEUM:	Mid Feb to end Oct.
BLISTS HILL OPEN AIR MUSEUM:	10am to 5pm.
ROSEHILL HOUSE:	Mid Feb to end Oct. 11am to 5pm.
TOURIST INFORMATION CENTRE:	at Toll House. Tel: 0952 882753 also Shopping Mall Telford Mon-Sat Tel: 0952 505370 extn 16.

Appendix 3: Much Wenlock

MUCH WENLOCK is a delightful little town that has not outgrown its strength and newer housing in the area has not diminished the heritage of the past. The modest size of the town makes practical an exploration of at least some of its places of interest in combination with some of the walks described.

The town is a mixture of half timbering, limestone and brick, and since many of the old properties are in very good order, the town repays a gentle stroll. Some of the buildings have been "labelled" by the local historical society and interesting reading they make. Ashfield Hall for example, is believed to be the site of ..."St John's Hospital in the 13th century for lost and naked beggars...." it has served as an inn, a private residence and offered hospitality to Charles I during the Civil War when he was on passage from Shrewsbury to his Oxford headquarters.

A particularly careful restoration is in hand on the beautifully timber-framed home of John and Mary Raynalds which bears their name and the date 1682. Barclays bank is housed in a black and white building that was once the Falcon Inn and there are other old inns still continuing in business.

The many arched and jettied Guildhall dates from 1540 with later additions and its handsome upper storey is still used for the Magistrates' Court. Its lower floor served as a corn market, with livestock being brought into the town each Monday. The town's history as a trading centre dates back to the early part of the 13th century and probably much earlier. Trade and pilgrims would have been attracted by the presence of the religious foundations, as indeed is the modern day tourist. It must have been a busy market centre for a notice of 1850 warns of the penalty that might be expected by any thoughtless enough to obstruct the way.....a sort of nineteenth century parking ticket......"Waggonners and others, Notice is hereby given that under the 34th bylaw in force in the Borough of Wenlock every person who shall on any Monday being market day between the hours of nine o'clock in the morning and six o'clock in the evening drive any waggon or cart, empty or laden

The Guild Hall, Much Wenlock

with coals, stone, lime or bricks or other materials, such waggon or cart not being used for the purpose of taking goods to or from Much Wenlock market through, along Smith Street or such part of High Street that lies between Spittle Street and the Fox Inn in the town of Much Wenlock in the said Borough shall be liable to a penalty of not more than £5 or less than one shilling for every offence, and such fine will be strictly enforced from and after the day of this notice by order of the Mayor. R.C.Blakeway Town Clerk 16th Sept 1850".

There is a record in the Borough's minute book of some of the costs associated with the building......"Paid to Richard Dawley for building the Court House, £13. 6. 8. and paid to Edward Brook for the Belfry with lead, fourteen shillings and four pence. Paid for the carriage of shingles to the court house 1/6d. Paid for wine to the various men for reward four shillings and nine pence"......must have been quite a celebration!

WENLOCK PRIORY

THE PRIORY owes its origins to a Mercian King, Merewalk, who placed his daughter Milburgha in charge as Abbess in 682AD. Quite how she came to be canonized does not fully emerge, quite possibly sainthood came more easily in those distant days, but she seems to have achieved considerable popularity and her name crops up elsewhere in the county. Under her guidance - a period that lasted some thirty years - the foundation flourished and popular legend credited her with miraculous works. She was buried within her Priory and in later years a shrine was built to which the usual crop of pilgrims came to make their devotions or look for benefits.

A well, still to be seen in the town, carries the saint's name and water from it was once said to cure eye diseases. Many other wells elsewhere, at Malvern for example, have a similar reputation and perhaps the waters did have soothing qualities. Another piece of folklore associated with the well extended into the last century. It took place on the Thursday in Holy Week when the unattached young ladies of the town, would meet at the well in the hope of ending their single state. It was their custom to throw bent pins into the well, at the same time wishing for the man of their dreams to make an early appearance. Meanwhile, the young men who might be expected to be the answer to these maidenly desires would have been encountered swigging beer brewed from rain water which had been collected from the church roof. The logic of all this escapes me, but that is no reason to spoil a good story!

There is nothing to be seen of Milburgha's original foundation. It was succeeded by a Cluniac foundation. The Priory remains that we visit today were the work of Prior Humbert during the first half of the 13th century. The prior was a confidante of Henry III and was entrusted with various diplomatic missions both overseas and with the neighbouring Welsh. The dissolution of the monasteries put an end to Wenlock Abbey as it did for many others. Not that the monks were badly treated, in common with other such institutions their adherents were found places in the church elsewhere or pensioned off with not ungenerous settlements.

Today only the birds remain to sing evensong where the several religious communities performed the offices of the day. Despite the dereliction following the reformation the site is still impressive and

Wenlock Abbey

it is not difficult to imagine it as it was in days of its glory. An artist's impression of the Priory can be seen in the town's museum which adds flesh to the bare bones of its present skeleton.

THE PARISH CHURCH

THE CHURCH can claim a history dating from circa 680 when it was built for the nuns of the Abbey. The foundation's first Abbess, Milburgha, was buried in the Lady Chapel. Her bones and coffin came to light in 1101 and were moved to the newly built Norman Priory. The nave was the work of the Cluniac monks about 1150 but the sporting man may be expected to take rather more interest in the memorial to Dr William Penny Brookes who is credited with being one of the movers in the revival of the Olympic Games.

MUCH WENLOCK MUSEUM

AMONGST THE many exhibits giving the flavour of the town's history is a display devoted to the good Doctor Brookes and detailing the formation of the Wenlock Olympian Society which from then on provided a field of athletic competition which attracted attention beyond the bounds of the small Shropshire town. So much so that Brooks is credited by some as being the true architect of the revival of the Olympic Games.

Certainly it was the big event of the year in the Wenlock area. The 27th meeting in 1877 offered a first prize of £5 for flat tilting, £1 for pole leaping and the successful competitor in a 200 yard race for boys aged under 14 received five shillings. The victor in a three mile bicycle race could claim £5 and tilting at the ring on horses over two flights of hurdles was handsomely rewarded with a prize of £10.

Old photographs of the games reveal that they were taken very seriously indeed. The spirit of Merrie England was about and the champion tilter is shown with his herald standing by a tournament tent in the style apparently favoured by the medieval jousters. This was no rough and ready knock about to please the village on an autumn afternoon; the participants turned out in appropriate dress and the herald is shown in the costume of his calling of the 16th century, with maroon cape, fine shirt, handsome boots and topped off by a plumed hat.

The pentathlon was one of the events and it seems the games founder was a considerable competitor in his own right. A painting shows him with the pentathlon blue riband and an olive crown.

Appendix 4: Ludlow

LUDLOW IS the jewel in the crown of Shropshire's heritage for it is surely one of the finest small towns in the country with great architectural riches. Let me quote one impressive statistic - the town has no fewer than 469 listed buildings, proof of the pleasures that are waiting to be enjoyed by visitors with time to make a leisurely exploration of this hill-top town. The exploration is greatly aided by the use of the excellent Ludlow Walks leaflet produced by the Civic Society which has also been responsible for fixing blue plaques to a number of buildings of special interest.

The quality of its buildings reflects the town's prosperity which was aided by geographical, political and economic factors. Ludlow's long development began following the Norman invasion of England when the new masters of the country built a series of castles as part of the strategy to secure their western borders against the Welsh. The building of the castle triggered the development of the town. The security of living beneath the castle walls must have had a considerable appeal.

The strategic importance of Ludlow also made it a focal point for trade and the town developed as a market and a prosperous centre of the woollen industry. Today's Castle Square is part of the 12th century market place which extended from the Castle to the Bullring. It was a rich Ludlow clothier that bought Stokesay Castle in the thirteenth century. (See Walk 15) The town's further prosperity was ensured by the Castle's establishment as the seat of the Council of the Marches. This administrative body grew in power and in the reign of Henry VIII had its permanent quarters in the castle from which it continued to rule Wales and the border counties of Shropshire, Herefordshire, Worcestershire and Gloucestershire until it was abolished in 1689.

This "regional seat of government" made Ludlow an even busier place and some of Ludlow's well known buildings date from this time when substantial houses were built for those engaged in the business of the Council. Later, Ludlow, like Worcester, was an important centre of the glove industry.

Ludlow - market, church and the Clee Hills - from Ludlow Castle

Ludlow is set high above the River Teme with its streets rising to the centre of the town developed around the castle, market place and church. The "classic" view of Ludlow which is so often seen in the guides to Britain is that from Whitcliffe - a handsome prospect that is enjoyed to the fullest when the sun has moved into the west to properly light the scene. Above the trees rise the walls of the castle and the tall tower of the fine parish church with Clee Hills providing a backdrop that confirms this as one of the finest views of a town and its countryside. It is at its most dramatic not on a day of clear blue skies but when clouds driven by a strong wind produce alternating periods of shade and light. Sometimes with just the castle or church tower lit, or the town standing blackly against the brightness of the distant hills, a scene that may soon, like a photographic negative be reversed.

Then there is the river, best enjoyed from the 15th century Ludford Bridge. Here the fast flowing waters, released from the restraints of the weir, come tumbling down over a rocky course. A pleasure that may be enhanced by a bright flash of colour as a kingfisher darts upstream to another perch. The Youth Hostel is in Ludford Lodge, delightfully situated by the bridge.

There is another fine view of the river from the topmost tower of the Castle, here above the weir this is Shropshire's counterpart to the view of the Avon from Warwick Castle, with swallows skimming low over the water, the splash of oars from little boats and the paddles of brightly coloured canoes. It is also in a measure reminiscent of Richmond, that splendid Yorkshire stronghold with the Swale running beneath the castle walls.

The strength of the castle is apparent even in its partial roofless state, with its strategic position on the Marches commanding the river, the north-south road and the approaches from the west. A special feature of interest is the round tower of the chapel of St Mary Magdalene, one of only a handful of circular churches in the country.

Castles are by their very nature exciting places, an irresistible magnet quickly bringing all sorts of images to the mind. Ludlow is very satisfactory in this respect, with its curtain wall, high ramparts and keep, with little dark passages linking the great halls and winding stone stairways.

Royalty would have been entertained here, perhaps their favours sought, or maybe the boot was on the other foot and the king was here to seek to assure himself of the undying loyalty of the lord who held the castle. In the Great Chamber the eyes of past monarchs gaze stonily down upon us and maybe the cold stones will encourage a little shiver when we read that it was the all powerful owner Roger Mortimer that was responsible for the horrific murder of Edward II at Berkeley Castle in 1327. Three years later the hand of retribution struck and Mortimer was hung, drawn and quartered at Tyburn.

The Castle is associated with another contentious chapter in the history of the monarchy. The "Princes in the Tower", the alleged illegitimate Edward V together with his younger brother, lived here as Prince of Wales until his accession to the throne in 1483 at the age of 12. Their removal to the Tower of London and subsequent murder, has engaged both historians and writers of historical dramas over a long period.

Of all the buildings in the town the most photographed is the handsome half timbered Feathers Hotel, once the home of Rees Jones, a Pembrokeshire man who came to the town as an attorney at the Council of the Marches. His initials are to be found on the lock plate and the fine carvings on the door lintels demand attention. His home became an inn in 1670, with later alterations including the addition of a balcony for electioneering.

The Feathers, which has been described as a treasure house, inside and out, is not the town's oldest inn. That honour falls to The Bull Inn. Approached from the little alley from the churchyard it presents the familiar film set image of an inn, with jettied buildings and a wide entrance through which coaches would bring their passengers. Amongst the town's many handsome buildings must be numbered the double jettied premises at the corner of Broad Street.

The town has a little network of alleys, short cuts well used by the residents which the visitor gradually discovers. You may return again and again to Ludlow and each time see something different, elaborate little carvings on buildings previously missed. Places like the Reader's House, a tall three-storied wood framed building behind the church, with leaded lights, an iron studded door and carved arch above the window grill.

The most prominent building on the skyline is the cathedral-like church which has attracted the attention of many famous writers of the past. The church guide is the most detailed I have seen of any

The Feathers Inn, Ludlow

parish church and deservedly so with so much to be seen. Not the least the monuments which reflect the period of the Council of the Marches. There is the colourful monument erected by Edward

Waties to commemorate himself and his wife Martha who died in 1629. This favoured position in the chancel reflects his membership of the Council of the Marches and his marriage.

There is a fine tomb to Edmund Walter and his wife Mary. Edmund Walter was Chief Justice of the Shires in South Wales and a member of His Majesty's Council for the Marches of Wales. Rivalling this is the tomb of Sir Robert Townshend and his wife Alice. He too was a Justice of the Council of the Marches.

The church is dedicated to St Laurence and the east window depicts a series of events in the life of the saint including his repeated beatings and torture and martyrdom on the gridiron.

The choir stalls are of great interest with elaborate carvings and numerous misericords which depict a wide variety of subjects. These include a fox disguised as a bishop preaching to a flock of geese. A mermaid with the traditional comb and mirror, a woman with extravagant horned headwear and retribution falling upon an ale-wife notorious for giving short measure. All very popular subjects for the photographer.

Adjoining the church are The Hosyer's Almshouses, a handsome town-hall like building originally built in 1486 and restored and extended in 1758. Other buildings which will take the interest are the Buttercross, rebuilt in 1743 and which once housed the Bluecoat Charity School, and the Tolsey. A plaque on the wall records "The Tolsey, 15th century acts and charters of Edward IV and VI governed the taking of tolls on market goods, Court of Pied Powder, (or dusty feet) for the summary justice of market offences such as dishonest trading and restrictive practices. Extensively repaired in 1624 when 2500 pinnes were needed. Saved from demolition and restored 1963/1964 by the efforts of the owner, Mrs Hardy, the Ludlow Town Council, Shropshire County Council, Historic Buildings Trust and the Ludlow Society." It now does duty as a fruit and vegetable shop.

Most towns have their museums and Ludlow is no exception with an array of exhibits telling something of its history, from the Norman Conquest. Under the heading of crime and punishment we are introduced to some barbaric items. A torture mask of about 1630 which was discovered hidden in the castle wall. The gradual tightening of screws was intended to extract information from prisoners with a branding iron used to leave permanent scarring on the face. We are informed that the Court of the Marches was expected to torture "when they should think convenient those suspected of treason, murder or felonies". A man trap dating from 1710 used to deter poachers and the like, hardly seems less kindly and only became illegal in the middle of the last century. (A strong inducement to walkers of the day to keep to the path.)

One man's punishment was another man's living and the museum quotes from accounts, for example in 1565 a rope to bind prisoners and to hang a man was charged at sixpence.

In 1569 a charge of 24 pence is recorded for whipping vagabonds whilst a few years later a Richard Hall is given 24 pence for nailing three men to the pillory. In the next century a man that carried a ladder to and from the execution was rewarded with fourpence.

A whole variety of items build a picture of life in the town - a Victorian sitting room with a lady in the dress of 1885. Old photographs showing the fire brigade with its hand drawn pumps and the laying of the first electricity cable in 1906. The sensation of 1913 was an aeroplane display. In 1817 a Signor Riviletto visited the town with what can best be described as a one man band. His performance was advertised to end with Rule Brittania and God Save the King upon eight instruments at one time!

The walker giving his boots a day off will find much of absorbing interest in Ludlow.

PLACES TO VISIT

ST LAURENCE'S CHURCH:	Open daily throughout the year.
THE CASTLE:	Open daily February to November.
DINHAM HOUSE:	A former town house now a craft and exhibition centre. Open daily February through to end December.
MUSEUM:	Open daily June - August and Mondays to Saturdays, April, May and September.
VIEWPOINT:	Whitcliff Common. approach over Dinham Bridge.

CICERONE GUIDES

Cicerone publish a wide range of reliable guides to walking and climbing in
Britain - and other general interest books

LAKE DISTRICT - General Books
LAKELAND VILLAGES
WORDSWORTH'S DUDDON REVISITED
THE REGATTA MEN
REFLECTIONS ON THE LAKES
OUR CUMBRIA
PETTIE
THE HIGH FELLS OF LAKELAND
CONISTON COPPER A History
LAKELAND - A taste to remember (Recipes)
THE LOST RESORT?
CHRONICLES OF MILNTHORPE
LOST LANCASHIRE

LAKE DISTRICT - Guide Books
CASTLES IN CUMBRIA
WESTMORLAND HERITAGE WALK
IN SEARCH OF WESTMORLAND
CONISTON COPPER MINES
SCRAMBLES IN THE LAKE DISTRICT
MORE SCRAMBLES IN THE LAKE DISTRICT
WINTER CLIMBS IN THE LAKE DISTRICT
WALKS IN SILVERDALE/ARNSIDE
BIRDS OF MORECAMBE BAY
THE EDEN WAY

NORTHERN ENGLAND (outside the Lakes
THE YORKSHIRE DALES A walker's guide
WALKING IN THE SOUTH PENNINES
LAUGHS ALONG THE PENNINE WAY
WALKS IN THE YORKSHIRE DALES (3 VOL)
WALKS TO YORKSHIRE WATERFALLS
NORTH YORK MOORS Walks
THE CLEVELAND WAY & MISSING LINK
DOUGLAS VALLEY WAY
THE RIBBLE WAY
WALKING NORTHERN RAILWAYS EAST
WALKING NORTHERN RAILWAYS WEST
HERITAGE TRAILS IN NW ENGLAND
BIRDWATCHING ON MERSEYSIDE
THE LANCASTER CANAL
FIELD EXCURSIONS IN NW ENGLAND
ROCK CLIMBS LANCASHIRE & NW
THE ISLE OF MAN COASTAL PATH

DERBYSHIRE & EAST MIDLANDS
WHITE PEAK WALKS - 2 Vols
HIGH PEAK WALKS
WHITE PEAK WAY
KINDER LOG
THE VIKING WAY
THE DEVIL'S MILL (Novel)
WHISTLING CLOUGH (Novel)
WALES & WEST MIDLANDS
THE RIDGES OF SNOWDONIA
HILLWALKING IN SNOWDONIA
ASCENT OF SNOWDON
WELSH WINTER CLIMBS
SNOWDONIA WHITE WATER SEA & SURF
SCRAMBLES IN SNOWDONIA
ROCK CLIMBS IN WEST MIDLANDS
THE SHROPSHIRE HILLS A Walker's Guide
SOUTH & SOUTH WEST ENGLAND
WALKS IN KENT
THE WEALDWAY & VANGUARD WAY
SOUTH DOWNS WAY & DOWNS LINK
COTSWOLD WAY
WALKING ON DARTMOOR
SOUTH WEST WAY - 2 Vol
SCOTLAND
SCRAMBLES IN LOCHABER
SCRAMBLES IN SKYE
THE ISLAND OF RHUM
CAIRNGORMS WINTER CLIMBS
WINTER CLIMBS BEN NEVIS & GLENCOE
SCOTTISH RAILWAY WALKS
TORRIDON A Walker's Guide
SKI TOURING IN SCOTLAND

THE MOUNTAINS OF ENGLAND & WALES
VOL 1 WALES
VOL 2 ENGLAND

*Also a full range of guidebooks
to walking, scrambling, ice-climbing,
rock climbing, and other adventurous
pursuits in Europe*

---

*Other guides are constantly being added to the Cicerone List.
Available from bookshops, outdoor equipment shops or direct (send for price list)
from CICERONE, 2 POLICE SQUARE, MILNTHORPE, CUMBRIA, LA7 7PY*

CICERONE GUIDES

Cicerone publish a wide range of reliable guides to walking and climbing in Europe

FRANCE
TOUR OF MONT BLANC
CHAMONIX MONT BLANC - A Walking Guide
TOUR OF THE OISANS: GR54
WALKING THE FRENCH ALPS: GR5
THE CORSICAN HIGH LEVEL ROUTE: GR20
THE WAY OF ST JAMES: GR65
THE PYRENEAN TRAIL: GR10
TOUR OF THE QUEYRAS
ROCK CLIMBS IN THE VERDON

FRANCE / SPAIN
WALKS AND CLIMBS IN THE PYRENEES
ROCK CLIMBS IN THE PYRENEES

SPAIN
WALKS & CLIMBS IN THE PICOS DE EUROPA
WALKING IN MALLORCA
BIRDWATCHING IN MALLORCA
COSTA BLANCA CLIMBS

FRANCE / SWITZERLAND
THE JURA - Walking the High Route and
 Winter Ski Traverses
CHAMONIX TO ZERMATT The Walker's Haute Route

SWITZERLAND
WALKS IN THE ENGADINE
THE VALAIS - A Walking Guide
THE ALPINE PASS ROUTE

GERMANY / AUSTRIA
THE KALKALPEN TRAVERSE
KLETTERSTEIG - Scrambles
WALKING IN THE BLACK FOREST
MOUNTAIN WALKING IN AUSTRIA
WALKING IN THE SALZKAMMERGUT
KING LUDWIG WAY

ITALY
ALTA VIA - High Level Walkis in the Dolomites
VIA FERRATA - Scrambles in the Dolomites
ITALIAN ROCK - Selected Rock Climbs in
 Northern Italy
CLASSIC CLIMBS IN THE DOLOMITES
WALKING IN THE DOLOMITES

OTHER AREAS
THE MOUNTAINS OF GREECE - A Walker's
Guide
CRETE: Off the beaten track
Treks & Climbs in the mountains of RHUM &
PETRA, JORDAN
THE ATLAS MOUNTAINS

GENERAL OUTDOOR BOOKS
LANDSCAPE PHOTOGRAPHY
FIRST AID FOR HILLWALKERS
MOUNTAIN WEATHER
MOUNTAINEERING LITERATURE
THE ADVENTURE ALTERNATIVE

CANOEING
SNOWDONIA WILD WATER, SEA & SURF
WILDWATER CANOEING
CANOEIST'S GUIDE TO THE NORTH EAST

CARTOON BOOKS
ON FOOT & FINGER
ON MORE FEET & FINGERS
LAUGHS ALONG THE PENNINE WAY

(cp) CICERONE PRESS

*Also a full range of guidebooks
to walking, scrambling, ice-climbing,
rock climbing, and other adventurous
pursuits in Britain and abroad*

*Other guides are constantly being added to the Cicerone List.
Available from bookshops, outdoor equipment shops or direct (send for price list)
from CICERONE, 2 POLICE SQUARE, MILNTHORPE, CUMBRIA, LA7 7PY*

Printed in Gt. Britain by
CARNMOR PRINT & DESIGN
95-97 LONDON RD. PRESTON